Published in advance keeping in view the current situation

Some thoughts towards law reforms on the topic of

AF660985

Terrorism

and on the topic of

Dishonoured Cheques

Excerpts from the forthcoming work

Justice, Courts and Delays

by

Arun Mohan
Sr. Advocate

Universal
Law Publishing Co. Pvt. Ltd.

2009 Edition

ISBN : 978-81-7534-750-2

© Reserved with the author

No part of this publication can be reproduced or transmitted in any form or by any means, without prior permission of the Publishers.

Published by
UNIVERSAL LAW PUBLISHING CO. PVT. LTD.
C-FF-1A, Dilkhush Industrial Estate,
(Opp. Hans Cinema, Azadpur) G.T. Karnal Road,
Delhi-110 033
Tel : 011-27438103, 27215334, 42381334
Fax : 011-27458529
e-mail *(For sales inquiries)* : sales@unilawbooks.com
e-mail *(For editorial inquiries)* : edit@unilawbooks.com
Website : www.unilawbooks.com

Recommended citation: *Some thoughts towards law reforms on the topic of Terrorism. Some thoughts towards law reforms on the topic of Dishonoured Cheques. Excerpts from the forthcoming work 'Justice, Courts and Delays'*, Arun Mohan (New Delhi: Universal Law Publishing Co. Pvt. Ltd., 2009)

This publication is being sold on the condition and understanding that the information, comments, and views it contains are merely for guidance and reference and must not be taken as having the authority of, or being binding in any way on, the author, editors, publishers, and sellers, who do not owe any responsibility whatsoever for any loss, damage, or distress to any person, whether or not a purchaser of this publication, on account of any action taken or not taken on the basis of this publication. Despite all the care taken, errors or omissions may have crept inadvertently into this publication. The publishers shall be obliged if any such error or omission is brought to their notice for possible correction in a future edition. In the case of binding defect, misprint, missing pages, etc., the publishers' liability is limited to replacement of the defective copy within one month of its purchase by a copy of the same edition or reprint. All disputes are subject to the jurisdiction of competent courts in Delhi.

Printed at Sita Fine Arts, New Delhi.

Publisher's Note

Delays in justice delivery has been a problem for long. Universal is proud that they have been entrusted with the task of placing Mr. Arun Mohan, Sr. Advocate's forthcoming work 'Justice, Courts and Delays' before the readers. It is an unusual project, which has been in process for well over a decade – unusual in the sense that it is a writing preceded by extensive research on the functioning of our laws, substantive and procedural, and justice system, with the broader goal of removing delays.

Despite its length (about 5,000 pages), the work does not purport to be a mere statement of the existing law, but seeks to analyse the existing law, particularly procedural, with a view to: (1) make the best of the existing procedures and practices; and (2) put forward thoughts so as to enable the lawyers, the courts and even the public involved in the court cases, to further develop these thoughts for improvement in our laws and systems. The proposals and the reasoning put forward are only for consideration and further thinking, and the author's task is limited to that.

A public service project by Mr. Arun Mohan, a Senior Advocate of long standing and wide experience at Bar, and written in a manner for the layman and the learned alike, it has been presented in a slightly offbeat manner, replete with practical illustrations, all with the sole objective of helping reduce delays. The work is to be made available at a very low price so as to be affordable by the typical party who goes to the court and is otherwise affected by delays.

Spread over four volumes, the first two volumes are slated to be released shortly, while the remaining two will follow thereafter. A highly abridged version will be next followed by a translation in Hindi and other regional languages.

In the meantime, because of the current situation and the need to make available to the legal fraternity and the public the discussion on two issues (which otherwise fall in the third volume), these topics are being published as a booklet (excerpts) in advance. They will, of course, form part of the main work.

Accordingly, this booklet places before the readers Topic 10 and sub-topic 3 of Topic 14 of Chapter 10 (Criminal Law & Procedures), and sub-topic 3 of Topic 8 of Chapter 8, which address issues of Terrorism and Dishonoured Cheques. The Table of Contents of the main work has also been excerpted, more to give an idea of the context in which the two topics excerpted here have been written. There are some cross-references to other portions of the work, which have been left blank (with a ~), for it was found practical not to disturb the near finalised and complete pattern of the work.

The topic of Terrorism, which is herein excerpted, is not an analysis of the statute or case law. This topic was written long before the recent Mumbai episode, and was revised in the aftermath of the unfortunate event. This work is more of an identification and analysis of the problem, and a collection of thoughts and proposals, which could be considered in formulating our policies in that regard. The problem being what it is, and the subject being one where a perfect solution will not be easy, it is clarified that these are only thoughts for the purpose of getting more minds to think and work together on what should be the reform in our laws to tackle the menace, increase the efficiency of the system, and generally reduce crime.

'Dishonoured Cheques' is the subject discussed in sub-topic 3 of Topic 14 of Chapter 10 (Criminal Law and Procedures), which is titled 'Offence-Specific Tailoring of Procedures'. It takes a complaint case under Section 138 of the Negotiable Instruments Act for a dishonoured cheque as the basis for discussion, which begins from para 12 and continues till para 147. The remaining part of sub-topic 3 also argues a case for offence-specific tailoring of procedures by taking the example of other offences and has not been excerpted. A companion note / discussion (from sub-topic 3 of Topic 8 of Chapter 8) on the use of post-dated cheques as security in replacement of the traditional promissory note, and also the misuse, has been excerpted thereafter.

The contents of the work are just the thoughts that the author places towards reform in law and it is for the enlightened readers and others to use them as a platform to further develop them so that the collective effort on this score can help us as a nation to provide for ourselves the best of laws and systems.

February 28, 2009 Universal Law Publishing Co. Pvt. Ltd.

Excerpts from Justice, Courts and Delays

Contents of this Booklet

Chapter 10

Criminal Law and Procedures

Topic 10 Terrorism

10. Terrorism

- - -

Chapter 10

Criminal Law and Procedures

Topic 10 Terrorism

10. Terrorism

1 The last topic discussed was 'Organised Crime'. In para ~ thereof, it was pointed out that 'Terrorism' is a species of crime, but perhaps a mutant and more virulent form of it. The difference lies not only in the gravity and barbarity of the crime but also in the motive and the societal havoc towards which it is directed. 'Terror' means a state of intense fright or apprehension, or stark fear. Similarly, 'terrorism' means the systematic use of terror as a means of coercion; creating an atmosphere of threat, violence or panic through an organised group or mercenaries, having misplaced political or ideological impulsions.

2 It is not easy to give a precise definition of 'terrorism' or lay down what constitutes 'terrorism' (see para 186 *et seq*). It may however be possible to describe it as the use of violence when its most important result is not merely the physical and mental damage to the victim but also the prolonged psychological effect it produces, or has the potential of producing, on society as a whole. Apart from injury to the victims, the damage that terrorism causes to the socio-economic fabric of civil society is colossal. It could even take the shape of a war by proxy.

1. A threat to the nation and to the society – Causes and effect

3 Terrorism has now become a global menace, and is the biggest threat today for many countries. The terrorists are waging wars against the sovereignty of nations, or against a race or community, in order to create an embryonic imbalance and nervous disorder in society on being stimulated or instigated by national or trans-national hardcore criminals or secessionists. Resultantly, the security and integrity of the countries concerned is gravely imperilled, and law and order is disrupted. The cult of the bullet is hovering over the globe, completely robbing it of rhyme and reason.[1]

4 Though violent behaviour is not new, present-day 'terrorism' in its full manifestation has assumed a different character and poses extraordinary challenges to the civilised world. Terrorism is faceless and soulless. It has no political establishment. It is not rooted to one geographical territory. It is an insidious network of tiny groups, fiercely dedicated or indoctrinated, and well trained in unconventional techniques. It is spread across the world, often lying dormant with perfectly legitimate fronts till operatives get the signal to act. Its object is to disintegrate societies and structured life that are not in consonance with, or are in conflict with, their ideologies and belief.

---

1 See *Kartar Singh vs State of Punjab* 1994-3 SCC 569,'621 = 1994 Cri LJ 3139.

5 Acts of terrorism not only affect (and have affected) the well-being of individuals but also the stability of the entire nation. It poses a threat to the economy and lifeline of nations as well. Wherever terrorism has struck, not only industry and commerce, but normal life too has been adversely affected. Entire families have been forced to flee and relocate themselves in other parts of the country, while those who cannot leave their homes, live in a state of constant fear of their lives.

6 The fallout of terrorist activity is so structured that it travels beyond the capacity of the ordinary law enforcement agencies to control under ordinary penal laws. What distinguishes 'terrorism' from other forms of violence, therefore, appears to be the deliberate and systematic use of coercive intimidation, carrying with it the implied threat of indiscriminate violence. More often than not, a hardened criminal today takes advantage of the situation and by donning the cloak of 'terrorism', seeks to achieve for himself acceptability and respectability in a particular segment of society because unfortunately, in most societies affected by militancy, a 'terrorist' is often projected as a hero or 'freedom fighter' by his group and other misguided elements.

7 India has been the victim of an undeclared war by the epicentres of global terrorism, aided and abetted by highly committed, resourceful and ruthless terrorist organisations. The terrorists can strike at will, kill at will, and choose the time and venue of their attack. The increased frequency of terror attacks has exposed the vulnerability of the Indian State. While government statistics may reveal one picture, it is generally perceived that in the last two decades, over a hundred thousand persons have lost their lives to terrorism and millions have suffered injury in other forms.

8 The main targets of terrorist strikes have been: (1) institutions of democracy; (2) economic nerve centres; (3) security or strategic installations; (4) symbols of national pride; (5) civilians, in order to generate terror and a fear psychosis; and (6) places of worship, with an intention to injure sectarian sentiment so as to whip up communal passions. Their objective is to create a feeling of insecurity with a view to pit the populace against the legally constituted authority.

9 Religious extremists often reject the authority of secular governments and view political and legal systems that are not based on their usually skewed religious beliefs, as illegitimate. At times, the extremist 'leaders' see constituted authority as reducing their stranglehold on a section of the populace. Some even view efforts towards modernisation as corrupting influences on 'traditional culture'. Yet others see terrorism as a tool to destroy the authority of the State.

10 Some analysts claim that a fair amount of cross-border terrorism and insurgency is deliberately designed; in any case, it is aided or tacitly

supported by those nations who have a political, economic or strategic interest in the law and order situation in a particular region remaining volatile, resulting in a retarded economic growth and continued instability. Terrorism hampers the development of nations affected by it, and reduces their chances of emerging as strong economies. This does away with the competition that such (interested) countries would have faced if the targeted economy worked to optimum levels with the support of a good law and order situation. Further, terrorism in other lands usually creates a lucrative market for arms and technology sales.

11 In many cases, terrorist organisations are funded by nations who display one face in the diplomatic world and a different face in the opaque corridors of power. Some others are said to view it as a mode of maintaining regional importance and supremacy, or strategic dominance, or as an instrument of State policy, or for 'regime change'. Whatever be the truth, the fact remains that terrorism is the biggest scourge humanity is faced with today.

12 Sometimes, terrorism and narcotics exist in tandem; in fact, an uneasy inter-dependency often arises between them. The profits from the latter are used to fund terrorist outfits and for buying arms and equipment; at times, even for providing logistic support. It causes injury to the physical and mental health of the populace. Acts of terrorism lead to the paralysis or negation of law & order, and this, in turn, facilitates the narco-business. At the same time, there are several terrorist outfits that have nothing to do with narcotics and receive funding from other sources such as voluntary and forced donations in the name of the so-called 'cause'. There also exist foreign 'sources' which contribute dedicated 'slush' funds towards terrorism.

13 It is estimated that security-related costs in countering terrorist activities over the past decade have exceeded a hundred thousand Crores, which could alternatively have been spent on essentials like education, health and housing. Added to this is the loss in terms of stifled economic growth, which is many times more in terms of real wealth.

2. Laws against Terrorism – TADA, POTA

14 Coming then to laws dealing with terrorism, earlier, acts of terrorism were dealt with by the ordinary criminal law, namely, the Indian Penal Code and a handful of other laws. However, it was soon realised that the penal laws fell short in dealing with the problem. The Penal Code and the prevailing criminal justice system were designed only to check individual crimes and occasional riots at local levels, and were not adequate to handle other far-reaching and well-planned crimes like terrorism. Resultantly, the law enforcement agencies failed to meet the challenges of tackling such crimes while operating under the normal laws of the land.

15 Prior to 1980, acts of terrorism were dealt with (apart from the Indian Penal Code) under the Explosive Substances Act [6 of 1908] and the Arms Act [54 of 1959]. The Unlawful Activities (Prevention) Act [37 of 1967] was also passed and amended from time to time. There was the infamous MISA,[2] which proved ineffective and was also thoroughly misused. It was repealed on 3.08.1978. In 1980, the National Security Act [65 of 1980] was enacted for countering the threat posed by insurgency, as well as for the maintenance of internal security. It was the first Indian statute specifically aimed at combating terrorism. Thereafter the Terrorist Affected Areas (Special Courts) Act [61 of 1984] was also enacted.

16 In the year 1985, the TADA[3] was introduced in the country. Although an anti-terrorism law meant for the protection of society, it was both tough and stern. However, it found (mostly by reason of improper use and misuse) little public support. Other difficulties were also being faced. In 1993, it was further extended for a period of two years by amending the duration of the original Act. Because of widespread criticism, it was extended no further and was allowed to lapse in 1995.

17 After the lapse of TADA, the situation as it emerged, once again, required suitable legislation for effectively combating terrorism, which task was undertaken by the Law Commission. In April 2000, it gave its 173rd Report on 'Prevention of Terrorism Bill, 2000'. The period that ensued saw a worsening of the situation not only in India, but also worldwide, wherefore immediate action was called for. What ensued were Ordinances No. 9 of 2001 and No. 12 of 2001, and then the Prevention of Terrorism Act [15 of 2002] – POTA for short – was enacted.

18 POTA was a comparatively well-drafted piece of legislation and, in any case, was badly needed, but if the framers of the statute had been given a freer hand, it could have been better. POTA, like its predecessor, found itself being improperly wielded. Criticism, some genuine and some misplaced, erupted. By [The] Prevention of Terrorism (Repeal) Ordinance [1 of 2004], POTA was repealed (21.09.2004). In any case, whether TADA, POTA or any other, a special law to combat terrorism had to be in place. The purpose was sought to be achieved by an Ordinance [2 of 2004] to amend The Unlawful Activities (Prevention) Act [37 of 1967]. Amendment Act 29 of 2004 followed. See also para 20.

19 To fight terrorism, at the international level, there have been many treaties, for example, the International Convention for the Suppression of Terrorist Bombings [1997]; International Convention for the Suppression of the Financing of Terrorism [1999], etc. There have been many U.N. Resolutions, including the Global Counter-terrorism Strategy [2006]. There is also the Council of Europe Convention of 2005.

---

2 The Maintenance of Internal Security Act [26 of 1971]

3 Terrorist and Disruptive Activities (Prevention) Act [28 of 1987]. Introduced as an Ordinance in 1985, it was enacted as a Statute in 1987.

20 After the recent Mumbai terror attack (26/11), the National Investigation Agency Act [34 of 2008] was enacted, and by Act 35 of 2008 [31.12.2008], further changes were carried out to the Unlawful Activities (Prevention) Act [37 of 1967] with the intention of framing a tough law against terror –almost on the lines of the TADA and the POTA. See para 182 *et seq*.

21 The discussion in this topic proceeds on principle and contains thoughts with long-range objectives in mind and does not seek to be a commentary on (or a critique of) the statute/s recently enacted. First and foremost, laws to combat terrorism have to be bold, innovative and free from many Constitutional restraints which other laws are subject to. A terrorist follows no rules when he attacks the innocent, often causing them a painful death, and so with the intention to create a cascading effect. Therefore, he and those who support him deserve to be dealt with in a manner that is free from constraints. The safeguard of Article 20 is not meant to protect foreign mercenaries, or those engaged in terrorist activities, even though they may be Indian citizens.

22 Laws made by the civilised, directed against traditional deviants are both insufficient and inappropriate for application to these elements. And when the State frames laws to protect itself from the terrorists, such laws are assailed on issues of human rights and Constitutional safeguards of the suspects and accused. Cases of false implication apart, one wonders whether such critics consider the fallen victims of yesterday and the potential victims of tomorrow – as also the millions of those who live under fear and will be forced to so live – as either being not human or simply not deserving of those very same human rights and Constitutional safeguards.

23 Critics have to keep in mind the larger interest of the nation. A person who, with the intent of threatening the integrity, security or sovereignty of India or striking terror among the people or any section of the people, does any act or thing by using bombs, dynamite and other sophisticated weapons, deserves no sympathy. His actions disentitle him to claim parity of treatment with an ordinary criminal. In today's world, the terrorist has to thank himself for forging his own fetters. He cannot complain that the provisions of law in that regard suffer from the vice of discrimination.

24 Thus, to contain the malaise of terrorism, what is first required is an efficient intelligence network, a highly trained and well-equipped counter-strike or commando force and, above all, a firm Government policy for dealing with terrorism. The next requirement is of stringent laws and efficient enforcement machinery that can effectively deal with all facets of terrorism in their entirety. The law will need to have new jurisprudential principles, and the principles of natural justice, right to equal treatment before law, and the right to be deemed innocent till proven guilty beyond reasonable doubt, would have, to some extent, be tailored.

3. Misuse of Anti-Terrorism Laws

25 There is another serious issue that must be addressed – complaints of the misuse of anti-terrorism laws (AT-laws for short). Use, and misuse, can be broadly segregated under the following heads:

1 genuine use, giving it a patina of misuse;

2 use of such laws against terrorists not proved to be so;

3 error of perception;

4 use against a criminal, but not meriting the use of anti-terrorism laws; and

5 use against an innocent person who, in any case, is not a terrorist, only to teach him a lesson or remove him as an opponent–in other words, deliberate false use.

The result of misuse has been that on the one hand, the 'punch' of such laws gets negated and on the other, there are cries to repeal these laws. Public support for these laws–and for those who enforce them–wanes.

26 The past has seen the authorities using stringent laws incorrectly or indiscriminately. This does incalculable harm to the system. The thumb rule is as the adage goes: 'The greater the use of such laws against a person not actually guilty of terrorism, the weaker is the law tomorrow'. At the same time, correct use which resulted in an acquittal for want of evidence cannot be termed as misuse, as it has often (and wrongly) been.

27 Whatever statistics the critics of the anti-terrorism laws may flaunt about the low conviction rates under these laws, the fact remains that many (though not all) of the accused were guilty but acquitted because adequate proof of guilt could not be made available. One may only ask whether a person who saw a terrorist act happen in front of his eyes would venture to give evidence (testimony) of it in court. If the answer is what it invariably is, this would provide one of the reasons for a low conviction rate. To give the status of 'falsely arraigned' to all those who were acquitted for want of evidence is improper.

28 Even though there could be an overlap between a 'terrorist' act and an ordinary criminal act, it is not the intention that every criminal should be tried under specially legislated laws, where the fallout of his activity does not extend beyond the normal frontiers of ordinary criminal activity. Every 'terrorist' may be a criminal, but every criminal cannot be given the label of a 'terrorist' simply to invoke the more stringent provisions of Terrorist laws.[4]

29 No doubt, to protect society from terrorism, it is essential to have laws that have sharp teeth, and systems for intelligence-gathering and investigation. Yet, it is the 'misuse' of such laws and systems for personal or political ends that renders them blunt and ineffective. On

---

4 *Hitendra Vishnu Thakur vs State of Maharashtra* 1994-4 SCC 602,'18 = AIR 1994 SC 2623,'9-30

the question of the misuse of laws and State agencies by the Government of the day, the Supreme Court in *Vineet Narain vs U.O.I.*[5] had noted:

> 16 ... No doubt, the overall control of the agencies and responsibility of their functioning has to be in the executive, but then a scheme giving the needed insulation from extraneous influences, even of the controlling executive, is imperative. ...

A decade has gone by. No such scheme has yet been implemented. A system and set-up which is susceptible to least misuse and enjoys public confidence needs to be put in place at the earliest.

30 It must be remembered that all laws derive strength not only from the authority of the State but also from the support of the people. Every instance of misuse only destroys or erodes public support, and denudes the law of its potency. Therefore, while strengthening the laws against terrorism, putting in place safeguards which both prevent and punish misuse is essential. Public cooperation is necessary to support the State in its fight against terrorism. However, there is a difference between 'bonafide error' on the one hand and 'intentional misuse' on the other, which may not be discernable today, but when the truth dawns – and as a result thereof, laws like this come to lose their force – it is posterity that suffers at the hands of terrorism.

31 An extraordinary situation calls for an extraordinary law, which is designed to meet and check such situations. It is one thing to say that the State must create and provide internal structures and safeguards against possible misuse or abuse of the statute, and altogether a different thing to say that because a law is liable to be misused, it should not have been the law (statute) at all. It is a truism that the wisdom of Man has not been able to conceive of a government with power enough to answer all its legitimate needs and, at the same time, be incapable of mischief.

4. Laws of a Special Kind

32 Terrorist acts cannot be equated with normal law and order problems, which are usually local in dimension. Terrorism does not respect any State or even national boundaries and is mostly cross-border in character. Despite its being an oft-used word, terrorism can be a nebulous concept and can elude a clear definition. It is a criminal act, which is much more than mere criminality. The fight against overt and covert acts of terrorism is not a regular criminal justice endeavour. Rather, such a fight is part of the defence of a nation and its society.

33 There may be death, injury, destruction of property or even deprivation of individual liberty in this process, but the extent and reach of the intended terrorist activity travels well beyond the pale of an ordinary crime punishable under the ordinary penal law of the land. Therefore, to effectively deal with terrorism, it needs laws of its own, and of a

5 1998-1 SCC 226,'43 = AIR 1998 SC 889

special kind, along with new approaches, techniques, weapons, and expertise. The history of anti-terrorism laws in the past has been noted in paras 15 to 19. In the absence of anti-terrorism laws, the laws against organised crime (discussed in Topic 9) have been invoked against terrorists, which is wrong. Equally wrong is to seek to use anti-terrorism laws against organised crime.[6]

34 True, there is some similarity, maybe an overlap, and they may operate in similar fields, but there is a fundamental difference between the two.[7] The difference essentially lies in their respective goals. In organised crime, it is money which is the goal while with terrorism, it is a misplaced sense of 'cause'. With organised crime, the fear or injury is directed against the victim from whom 'profit' or monetary gain can be expected. It is rarely directed against a target who is unlikely to or will not yield. Terrorism (except in special circumstances) is usually directed not against a particular individual, but for generally causing loss of life and destruction of public property with a view to spread fear among the public and cause erosion of the authority of the State.

35 Stated differently, in organised crime, the main lure is money whereas in terrorism, the lure is not money but a (misplaced) faith in a 'cause'. In organised crime, the perpetrator usually does not risk his own life for he wants to live for the day where he can use the illicit money, though he has no qualms to use another person's life for his own gain. In terrorism, the wrongdoer is usually 'ready to die' for the cause.

36 Of course, as a matter of perception, the organised criminal, treating his act as a profession, knows very well – at times more than a jurist – that what he is doing is against the law, whereas the terrorist believes that the present set-up, including the prevailing laws, is wrong and the acts that he is carrying out are sanctioned by the higher powers that be and are moral.

37 While in organised crime, there oft is a politico-bureaucratic nexus with criminals, in Terrorism, there usually is no such nexus,[8] but there is sympathy and tacit support from a section of the public who themselves are otherwise law-abiding (usually simple) people. The sympathisers contribute monies, though, at times, there is use of extortion or even receipt of finances from off-shore sources. When contributions from sympathisers to the cause run dry, the terrorists rely on drug-related organised crime as a source for funding their activities.

38 Such being the difference between the two, it is essential to treat a terrorist under anti-terrorism laws and by special courts as the laws and courts operating in normal times are not designed to cope with the class

6 except where the offender is involved in both or is using Organised Crime to fund/aid terrorism. It is the nature of the crime which should determine.

7 organised crime and terrorism

8 except in very few cases where some local political group is trying to use terrorism for its own survival or money-making

of crime that terrorism denotes. It is wrong to use the laws relating to organised crime for dealing with terrorists. The law has to keep statutes for the two, separate – separate in the sense that the statute will be separate; the rules will be separate; the investigation and prosecution agencies will be separate–though some element of overlap, as also inter-relationship between the agencies, cannot be avoided. It is essential to do so because, otherwise, primarily by reason of public response or reactions, the efficacy of the statute would be depleted.

39 In our federal set-up, law & order is a State subject, but to deal with terrorism, it needs a central set-up on many a score–and for reasons more than one. Thus far, terrorism has traditionally been under the purview of the States, with back-up from the Centre, but central intervention comes into play only on a specific request being made by the State or after the State's consent. It needs to be the other way around, namely, the responsibility being that of the Centre and supported by the States. Thus, comprehensive national counter-terrorism legislation and a highly professional intelligence and enforcement apparatus are imperative. The need of the hour is a centralised effort against terrorism.

40 Proceeding to another facet, Constitutional and human rights are meant for those who abide by the Constitution and respect humanity, and not for those whose only goal in life is to destroy human values and destabilise constitutional systems. This should be the guiding principle in framing laws against terrorism. Principles of criminal jurisprudence and constitutional provisions should only be viewed in that light. Citizens are bound to suffer some inconvenience in the fight against terrorism. Certain civil liberties are bound to be curtailed, but this should be treated as the price or a kind of a premium for insurance against terrorism. This could also be treated as society's contribution to saving the lives of those who otherwise would have fallen to the bullets and bombs of terrorists. See also Topic 7 supra for the discussion on Liberty, Human Rights and Crime Control.

41 The fight against terrorism requires multi-pronged action whereas common law is only one prong, and this prong (substantive and procedural law, including that relating to adjudication and punishment) will have to be not just stringent, but more importantly, also tailored and flexible. With severe punishment, often with a 'minimum', the courts insist (and rightly) on higher standards of proof. Many factually guilty are acquitted.

42 The statute/s against terrorism will have to do more than merely defining the offence, prescribing punishment and providing procedures for investigation, trial and adjudication. The coverage will have to be over very many areas, particularly creating and empowering intelligence and enforcement agencies, special courts and also spelling out the obligations of the general public and other various institutions. The

anti-terrorism law will also need a companion procedural Code on the lines of the existing Code [2 of 1974], but tailored to this specific need.

43 Alongside stringent anti-terrorism laws, there is also the need for laws to enforce public order. Its stringency will be something of a half-way house between the conventional criminal laws on the one hand and properly framed anti-terrorism laws on the other. A law such as this in place will prevent the utilisation of anti-terrorism laws for situations not really deserving their use, but the police, finding the conventional laws insufficient, nonetheless goes ahead using the available anti-terrorism laws. With appropriate laws (of intermediate stringency) in place, it will also enable the Special Courts (AT-Courts) to transfer or shift the matter to a court competent to deal with the accused under such law.

44 An anti-terrorism statute may stand alone, but it also needs to be synchronised with a number of other laws 'in support' so as to ensure the necessary Dos and Don'ts by the public. Many of these laws will be simple and routine (and relate to day-to-day life); nevertheless they will need to take into account terrorism-related matters and contingencies. After 9/11, USA, UK, Australia and some European countries have framed many new laws to deal with terrorism and its related aspects, particularly funding. A study of these plus inputs of our own officials, based on their experience, can be helpful in formulating laws to tackle terror.

45 As much of this chapter postulates, our laws, both substantive and procedural, call for offence-specific tailoring. Sub-topic 3 of Topic 14 seeks to explain this concept by a few illustrations. Anti-terrorism laws are an example of laws requiring specific tailoring, in both the substantive and procedural fields, as also constant updating.[9]

46 The fight is such where the totally innocent will find themselves being punished – at times, only for failing to take care – but to save lives, this has to be accepted. Unless the general populace exercises due care, terrorism cannot be effectively countered. Several of the citizens' other rights will need to be breached, but so long as the intention of the officers of the intelligence-gathering agencies and the investigating agencies is honest and bona fide, such aberrations will have to be tolerated in the interest of public safety.

5. Understanding the psychology of a terrorist

47 While devising laws to counter terrorism, the psychological bent of a terrorist is to be kept in mind. Terrorist activities cannot be equated with other criminal activities and neither does a terrorist's psychology depict a pattern similar to that of an ordinary criminal. Firstly, a terrorist is not always aiming to gain money. Secondly, while an ordinary criminal balances between the profits from crime and the chances of his escape, a

9 See the discussion on the making and updating of laws in Topic 2 of Chapter 9 at pp2~ supra.

terrorist has no such thoughts. Thirdly, a terrorist is fighting for what he perceives to be a just cause. In most cases, if not all, he goes ahead with a clear mind that what he is doing is, in his view, justified. Expatiating on it, in 99% cases, a criminal when embarking upon an offence knows that what he is going to do is against the law.[10] A terrorist, on the other hand, seeks to become the law.

48 The terrorist is not escaping the law, but taking it head-on in a fight. For him, nothing matters apart from the 'cause' he is committed to. He does not commit the act for himself. He has nothing to lose and readily accepts any injury to himself. The only thing he seeks is attention to his cause. He wants to be noticed for that reason alone. The terrorist wants more people watching rather than more people dead. He wants to see the authorities helpless in the face of his acts. Such being the difference in the basic thinking of a typical criminal and a terrorist, an analytical assessment of the latter is called for.

49 A deeper analysis into a terrorist's psychology would reveal that the terrorist does not usually seek the luxuries and opulence which typical criminals do; in fact, in many ways, he is detached not only from worldly material considerations, but even from personal relationships. His mind has either been indoctrinated or is being simply subsumed by someone else. Gullible youth are turned into merciless mercenaries.

50 The motive behind terrorism being wholly different than that of: (1) a petty criminal; (2) a criminal; (3) a dangerous criminal; and (4) an organised crime operator, the laws and methodology designed against the former (particularly for categories 1 and 2) just do not work against the terrorist. It will be a fundamental error to try and tackle terrorism with such laws or with the mindset that does not take the threat perception seriously. To tackle terrorism, a complete change in approach is required – be it in the area of surveillance and investigation, or adjudication and final punishment.

51 Terrorism is a criminal act that affects people far beyond the immediate victim. The strategy of the terrorists is to commit acts of violence that draws the attention of the local populace, the government, and the world to their cause. The terrorists plan their attack to obtain the greatest publicity, choosing targets that symbolise what they oppose. The effectiveness of the terrorist act lies not in the act itself, but in the public or government's reaction to the act. For example, the Mumbai attack killed a few hundred people who were the victims and also affected their kith and kin. But the designated target was the Indian populace and the government – and the billion plus watching the televised event and its aftermath. The perpetrators probably measured their 'success' by this consideration and the Government's ability (or otherwise) to retaliate.

10 The considerations that revolve in his mind have been analysed in sub-topics 3 & 4 of Topic 6 at pp~ supra.

52 There are three perspectives of terrorism: the terrorist's, the victim's, and that of the general public. Terrorists do not see themselves as evil. They believe they are some kind of heroic warriors, fighting for what they believe in, by whatever means possible. A victim of a terrorist act sees the terrorist as a criminal with no regard for human life. The general public's view is one of all-round deprecation, but there can also prevail stray components of sympathy or even admiration, depending on individual belief. This sympathetic view of terrorism has become an integral part of their psychological warfare and needs to be vigorously countered.

53 Terrorists seek 'soft' targets which are easier to attack–and are unlikely to abandon such a tactic against civilians even if it provokes all-round and worldwide condemnation. Changes in the tactics and techniques of terrorists have been significant, but even more significant is the growth in the number of causes and social contexts in apparent support of which terrorism is resorted to.

54 As research studies have shown, terrorism has often been an effective tactic in asymmetrical confrontations for the weaker side in a conflict, i.e., it is an unequal form of conflict. It confers coercive power with many of the advantages of military force at a fraction of the cost. Due to the secretive nature and small size of terrorist organisations, they often offer the established State no clear organisation to target or counter.

55 In some cases, terrorism is resorted to in order to carry on a conflict without letting the adversary realise the nature of the threat. Because of these characteristics, terrorism has become increasingly common among those pursuing extreme goals in various regions throughout the world. While the meaning of the word terror itself is clear, when it is applied to acts and the people carrying it out in the real world, it tends to obfuscate. Part of this is due to the use of terror tactics by some, at all levels in the social and political spectrum.

56 Distinctions of size and political legitimacy of the groups resorting to terror, raise questions as to what acts constitute terrorism and which do not. The concept of moral, human and other rights is frequently used as a contention to widen and blur the definition of terrorism. This is the reasoning behind the famous phrase 'One man's terrorist is another man's freedom fighter'. It is also a legacy of legitimising the use of terror by successful revolutionary movements after the fact.

57 The induction of most of the downtrodden, unemployed and semi-literate youth, by giving false promises or misguiding them, has always been a grave problem. Of late, some of those involved in acts of terror are no longer socially oppressed and victims of injustice where frustration has misled them into committing crimes of terror. Often, they are educated young men from comparatively affluent backgrounds. These indoctrinated youth have no alternative but to compulsorily obey the

orders or instructions of their leaders or else they will be caught by the police or exterminated at the instance of their own masters. This situation can be explained by three different components – the Producer and Director, the Actor and the Audience – where the first is the leader or the mastermind, the second is the indoctrinated one who comes forward as the visible terrorist, and the third is that section of the populace which acts as a sympathiser and admirer.

58 As already stated, terrorism cannot flourish without the support of those whose ideology it represents. There is a dualism that manifests itself here. Unfortunately, some even refer to terrorism in veiled terms as a 'freedom struggle', or a war against tyranny and oppression. So, on the one hand, we have bloodshed, destruction of life and property, breakdown of law and order, and on the other, people supporting such activities on moral, sympathetic, religious or ideological grounds.

59 The other part is that no terrorist can rise unless he has the following and support of a section of the populace, wherever situate. While their (supporters') innocence as citizens must be respected, it is this tacit support, which may even be as trivial as mere applause for his act, that ultimately contributes to the terrorist's activities. Therefore, some, if not all, responsibility for the terrorist's act must also lie with those who encourage him.

60 Organisational issues apart, and stated theoretically, a terrorist needs:

i ten persons' support directly;
ii a hundred more supporting partially;
iii a thousand more hero-worshipping him; and
iv many acquiescing in his acts out of fear or the inability to resist.

Therefore, going for or hitting only him (the terrorist) is pointless and, in practical effect, may, at times, even be counterproductive.

61 Looked at in another way, mass support – having its origin in 'mis-' or 'dis-' information coupled with indoctrination and utopian expectations – operates as the lifeblood of terrorism, and those in organisational control use every possible method, including contrived impoverishment and denial of education, to ensure that such a state of affairs continues.

62 Terrorism, its general form apart, is of late manifesting itself in a more sinister form. The World is witnessing what are technically called 'suicide attacks'. Here, the indoctrinated minds are not even afraid of sacrificing their own lives. It would appear that their minds have been 'programmed' to accomplish their objective, whatever be the cost. Indoctrination of young minds is thus posing formidable problems for which there is no immediate effective remedy available.

63 There being no punishment greater than the death penalty, it becomes all the more difficult to handle these 'suicide attackers'. But this does not mean that the law and society should throw up its hands in despair and rest content with a ring of armed guards around each important person, while the average citizen continues to live in fear and insecurity.

64 Once again, the proper approach perhaps would be to first understand the underlying psychology so as to work out the penal and social remedies required. Here, and as a first step, the attempt should be to apprehend and punish those who indoctrinate or assist in such acts. This, however, is not always practical or possible, therefore, for the next step–and quite contrary to traditional jurisprudence – there is a need to explore the feasibility of 'punishing'[11] those who motivated or misguided the suicide attacker or who the suicide attacker thinks will benefit from his act.

65 Fear of such 'penalty', instead of encouragement and support, will ensure dissuasion from those quarters that matter. Whatever be the cause and the source, identification thereof will help in tackling nascent terror. Unless the psychology of the terrorists (as also their manner of operation which is constantly changing) is understood and analysed, lawmakers cannot set about making appropriate laws.

6. A Basic Policy

66 In seeking to tackle the problem, certain fundamentals need to be discussed. Till now, society has paid a heavy price by adopting a soft approach towards terrorism. The errors of the past continue to haunt us as a society and will do so till a clear message is conveyed that we have changed. India is considered to be a soft target. A permanent policy – of "No Negotiation and No Surrender" whatsoever–has now become inevitable. To a terrorist (as also his organisation or followers) a 'no giving-in' attitude symbolises failure that is way beyond his expectation whereas a 'giving-in' attitude is the very 'success' desired by a terrorist and his cohorts.

67 Such 'giving-in' operates as a shot in the arm and only motivates terrorist organisations to commit further outrages. The approach of hitting back at the source, wherever it be located, by covert or overt operations will also have to be adopted, and for that it is necessary to identify not just the few men who come forward, but also the brains behind, the source of the resources and even the sympathisers. To inculcate such a realisation among the terrorists and their supporters, there is a need to adopt a strong policy as aforesaid and make it clear by action that all appropriate measures–even if they are viewed as harsh–shall be taken.

68 To take a sample, terrorists often take innocent people hostage in order to obtain the release of those arrested or facilitate escape from the scene

---

11 The sanctions here will have to be innovative, wide & varied and graded according to an ascending scale, and then carefully applied. Many actions at many times will have to be carried out in an extra-legal manner while maintaining a credible denial of being the force behind it.

of a terrorist strike or even possibly seek other demands. This is a problem which has been allowed to aggravate because of society's passive past attitude. Here again, the approach has to be one of: (1) No surrender or giving-in; (2) rescue operations with a risk to the lives of the hostage being a lesser (or even 'no') consideration; and (3) adequate retaliation at the (strongly) believed 'source' by setting aside the conventional norms of justice and fairness.

69 For dealing with the dead bodies of terrorists killed during suicide missions or hostage rescue operations, public opinion deserves a greater place as opposed to the cold print of International Conventions. Similarly, for the interrogation of those terrorists who are captured alive in such an operation, most of the conventions and 'rights' will have to be looked at differently and possibly even overlooked.[12] In short, these frontline terrorists in particular need to be paid back not only in the same coin but maybe in even harder currency.

70 This does not mean that law-enforcers take upon themselves the role of 'executioners', but only that in the case of terrorism, they act forcefully for the sake of effectively dealing with the situation in the interest of the larger population that is reeling under threat. It is prompt and effective executive action that is important, perhaps more important than strict laws that will tilt the scales. It would be better to err on the higher side and go a little out of the way against a few, than to leave the major part of the population under the shadow of death, only because principles came in the way. The thrust is not on becoming 'brutal' to eliminate brutality, but on at least taking effective action against such brutes.

71 A message has to be sent out that terrorism in any form is wrong and is against humanity, the price of which will one day be paid not only by the terrorist and his active supporters but also by those who indirectly aid him. Realisation must dawn that far from operating as a gain for the purported cause (or the people), terrorism will, in the long run, injure them as well. It is only when such realisation sets in, and the ones who thought themselves as being the 'beneficiaries' of terrorist acts come to think otherwise, would this problem be solved.

72 In any case, the message, as set out above, ought to be to the effect that:

- i The terrorist and the terrorist leader will be hit first;
- ii The direct supporters of terrorism will be hit next;
- iii The indirect supporters of terrorism will be tackled thereafter;
- iv Should the need arise, even those who hero-worship the terrorists may be made to bear the consequences of such actions; and
- v All in all, so long as anyone resorts to or even assists terrorism, the terrorists' demands will not be considered, let alone met.

---

12 for instance, the 1984 Convention against Torture and other Cruel, Inhuman and Degrading Treatment or Punishment

Unless these distinctions and factors are understood and given appropriate regard, effective laws to deal with and prevent terrorism cannot be framed. At the same time, a safeguard needs to be provided. A dividing line must be drawn between what is a terrorist act and what is only a protest under democratic principles.

73 Of course, it will be for the Government of the day to decide, and the policies of retaliatory action and hot pursuit may sound difficult or escalatory, but they have on many occasions in the past proven to be the most effective, and therefore, need to be considered more seriously, and not rejected out of hand.

74 The thought process of the offender in regard to general crime has been analysed in sub-topic 3 of Topic 6 supra, while the economic analysis carried out by him is analysed in sub-topic 4 thereof. Such analyses will help improve the criminal justice system generally, but it is understanding the psychology of a terrorist, and adopting a basic counter policy and remaining firmly committed to it, that will help thwart the menace of terrorism.

7. Arming the Executive

75 To protect the citizens against terrorism, the predominant role is of the executive wing of the government. Terrorism is not only bullets and bombs, it can take many forms and stages such as cyber attack on government or institution computer networks; pumping in fake currency or otherwise disrupting administration, to name a few. An anti-terrorism law is not a substitute for preventive intelligence or effective policing. It only provides for investigation and trial, and enables the State to punish a terrorist, including an abettor/conspirator, provided he is caught, which itself may be a remote possibility.

76 In the fight against terror, intelligence is all important. What then is 'intelligence'? Intelligence, in simple terms, means 'useful' information. For a company tendering for a government contract, information about its competitor's bid becomes intelligence. For a father looking for a match for his daughter, information about his health, assets, income, habits, etc. constitute intelligence. In order to contain terrorism, information of the persons involved and their activities is, in a broad form, intelligence.

77 Unlike most penal laws which define the offence and prescribe the punishment, the fight against terror will require attention on a very wide front. It is, therefore, addressed in two parts, the first being preventive, comprising intelligence-gathering and policing (detailed in this sub-topic 7); and the second (in the event of a terrorist attack or breach of law), of investigation, trial and punishment (detailed in sub-topic 8 infra). Only to emphasise on the difference in pattern from conventional crime control, roughly speaking, 95% of the effort & expense will go on the first and only 5% on the second. See the table in para 363 infra.

Some Fundamentals –1

78 In a crime there are usually five stages: (1) Motive; (2) Intention; (3) Preparation; (4) Attempt; and (5) Actual commission of the offence. Prevention can take place at any or all the first four stages. Prevention in the first two stages is achieved generally by inculcating correct societal and other values and specifically by appealing to the logical mental process of every human being of maximising gain and minimising cost (risks) while in the next three stages, it is punishment that is the laws' remedy. It is the fear of detection (and apprehension) and certainty of punishment which prevents the prospective criminal from going ahead with the crime. With most crimes, generally, in doing so, we treat punishment as the means to prevention, though this has its limitations and failings too, which have been addressed in other parts of this work.

79 However, with terrorism, the equations are wholly different. Terrorism is crime which can be prevented, but not in the same way as other crimes. The application of the general principles is not effective as fear of being arrested or of consequences to follow, is not a sufficient deterrent as these criminals are zealots with a high degree of motivation, pursuing goals which transcend normal calculations of gain versus costs. The difference in the psychology of a terrorist from that of an ordinary criminal has been addressed in sub-topic 5 (paras 47 to 50) supra.

80 To continue, unlike the traditional criminal who is generally alone in the process, though at times a few may conspire with him,[13] with terrorism, it is almost never a loner. There is a whole team (and supported by many) that is at work. The terrorist as we see is the tip of the iceberg or to be more precise, just the arrowhead with a long shaft and many tails behind – all of which are invisible. For one terrorist in front, it could be scores directly involved and a hundred indirectly concerned. Of course, by reason of logistics, of all these, only a few are in the 'know' of full details. The role of each is confined to a 'need to know' basis. In fact, it is on coordination of many acts – like the assembly of a jigsaw puzzle – that a terrorist act succeeds. There are also many others who could be having only a vague idea of the goings-on and nothing more.

81 Now, when a single person comes to the forefront, whether he succeeds or not is one question, but reaching to those behind him (directly and indirectly) is the more important task. The probability of apprehending and filing charges against the majority of those is remote, or as good as ruled out, as most escape detection. Therefore, it calls for efficient intelligence gathering, storage and processing systems to improve the situation in this regard – so that the possibility of many more of those involved being detected (and with evidence sufficient to charge them), and being prosecuted, increases. It is this which will operate to contain terror.

82 The intelligence-gathering will help broadly in two areas: (1) help thwart the attack; and (2) (in the event of one) enable proper investigations so as

13 The position is slightly differently with organised crime.

to book the culprits and thus improve chances of conviction followed by punishment. Looked at in another way there are two stages at which intelligence (information) may be utilised: (1) *pre*-event; and (2) *post*-event. The first part is intended to halt the attack in its tracks (i.e. before it is executed); and the second (which is a distinct one) is (after the event and as assisting the investigation agency) to collate and process the inputs and data collected and stored from the past so that within a few days of the event, it is known with reasonable accuracy: Who all were involved? How did they go about it? Where could the others involved be hiding? Where all is the evidence linking those involved to be found? Which other sources are to be tapped for further information?

83 Put differently, as the punishment means little – for the frontliners are ready to die, and the orchestrators and others involved have little likelihood of getting caught and facing prosecution[14] – the focus of the laws and the systems has to be on prevention and stopping a potential strike in its tracks. It is only when those who direct or in any way support the frontliners realise that they are also likely to be caught and punished, that punishment comes to work as a preventive.

84 Further, if the intelligence set-up is good, opportunity can be given to the arrowhead to proceed further while being covertly trailed, and just before the attacker is able to strike, the security forces are there to stop him. This, however, requires a command that is willing to take decisions and risks. It is active operational systems and a proactive approach that will ultimately help prevent terrorist activities.

85 Here, we must not mix up or confuse between an intelligence set-up and an investigating agency. Broadly compartmentalising, there will be:

1 the intelligence set-up with its many sub-parts, mostly faceless;
2 the visible face of the nodal intelligence set-up which interacts with the other government authorities, departments, utility/service provider companies, institutions, banks, municipalities, etc.;
3 the Special Security Force and the Crisis Management Group;
4 the investigation agency with its forensic support; and
5 special prosecutors and designated courts.

Each of these five are distinct and have to be so looked at.

86 Particularly, the intelligence agency is wholly different from the investigation agency. This sub-topic 7 addresses the first and the second (intelligence agency) in paras 87 to 136; and also the third (Special Security Force) in paras 137 to 157. Sub-topic 8 addresses the fourth (investigation agency and the related organisations) in the first part while the fifth (courts & procedures) is addressed partly in the later part of sub-topic 8 and then in sub-topic 9.

---

14 See discussion at pp3~ on the interaction between probability of detection and prosecution, certainty of conviction and severity of punishment.

More on Intelligence –2

87 It will be worthwhile to state here a few details with regard to intelligence-gathering and processing. Intelligence itself has two broad divisions: (1) Human Intelligence;[15] and (2) Technical Intelligence.[16] The syllabic abbreviations in use for these are: HUMINT – Human Intelligence; and TECHINT – Technical Intelligence. The latter is sub-divided into: SIGINT – Signals Intelligence; COMINT – Communications Intelligence; ELINT – Electronic Intelligence; and IMINT – Imagery Intelligence also known as Photo Intelligence (PHOTINT). There is also MASINT – which is very broad if not 'all'-encompassing; and OSINT – which refers to Open Source Intelligence.[17]

88 Actionable intelligence is divisible into two stages. The first is data collection whether by technical intelligence or by human intelligence, and the second stage is the processing of the data into information. The information thus gathered has to be processed, collated, analysed / assessed, portions re-verified and then selectively disseminated and utilised. For this, trained analysts who have the ability to extrapolate data are necessary to provide meaningful information. Further, the sources of information as also the methodology of collection have to be duly protected, i.e., we use it (the human intelligence and technical intelligence) in a manner that the source is not compromised.

89 The goings-on (activities) in society may be many and varied, but the electronic day and age enables their capturing and retention for long and at low cost. A quick sift through, and collation, of data and records, including surveillance images, is necessary in our fight against terrorism. The basic principle is that the bulk remains buried and should any further data (suspicious input) be received, the earlier part can be scanned and re-assessed in the light of the new information.

90 Most intelligence failures turn out to be the result of poor interpretation and assessment, rather than non-availability of information. Thus, it is the convergence that creates problems. A mine of data may be available, but lack of expertise or labour during processing leaves clear pointers unnoticed. The pieces have to fall into place for a picture to emerge and for the analysts to come to a conclusion. Thus focus on the second is important. There is also a need to focus on a proper use of intelligence rather than mere generation. Put simply (after an event), availability of data, a search through which increases the probability of apprehending the culprits and the persons behind them (after identifying, locating and isolating them), will, in turn, act as a preventive.

---

15 It refers to intelligence gathering by means of interpersonal contact as opposed to the more technical intelligence-gathering disciplines. It is intelligence derived from information collected and provided by human sources, and includes conversations with persons having access to pertinent information.

16 This includes intelligence gained from interception of voice, data or fax signals being transmitted by electronic means as well as through the Internet.

17 With the information explosion on the Internet in particular, there is a vast quantity of data openly available to anyone who can figure out how to search through it for the relevant bits and pieces buried amongst a mountain of chaff.

91 Terrorists have a high degree of motivation, wherefore intelligence collection as also 'halting a likely strike in its tracks' assumes a different dimension. The group carrying out the operation typically disengages and disappears after striking, leaving hardly any trace of its existence. Investigating agencies frequently encounter red herrings left by the terrorists to confuse the investigation and allow greater time to disband and escape. While we labour to fashion an effective counter-terrorism strategy, the terrorist groups usually display a marked advantage in adapting to newer technologies and modes of operation, allowing them to function more quickly and quietly compared to the resources of our intelligence apparatus.

92 A brief description of the intelligence set-ups in the country and their hierarchy is addressed in para 97 *et seq*. Reference may however be made here to the State Police which is at the bottom, and whose local intelligence units and networks remain the primary and critical source of information. This is because the investigation branch of the local police forces (as also the LIUs) places them in the unique position of being able to detect the emergence of terror networks or sleeper cells.

93 Unfortunately, they (the local police) remain the weakest link in the intelligence chain as these units carry the burden of acting more as colonial-style law enforcement agencies and not as modern units capable of organising proactive measures based on intelligence collation. In most States, there are manpower shortages in the police force – even below the numbers that are sanctioned. They are commonly afflicted with low morale, and face problems related to training and emoluments. There is lack of accountability, poor administrative discipline, mixed-up priorities and politicisation. The quality of the personnel could also be much better. Then, the police-criminal nexus and the pervasive corruption adds to it. In such a situation, it becomes virtually impossible to set up effective intelligence mechanisms.

94 Equally restricting has been the reluctance, and sometimes even refusal, of the intelligence and security agencies to share information among themselves. The Centre alone can receive intelligence from abroad, but the local sleeper cells and nodules are usually better known to the States' intelligence. In the absence of proper information sharing, the whole exercise becomes futile. Rivalries within intelligence agencies also tell upon their efficacy. Information comes from the grass-roots level, but it is inadequately collated and disseminated. Even if that is done, i.e., it is effectively processed, hardly any action is taken as a sequel thereto.

Saxena Committee Report –3

95 After the Kargil conflict, on 10.5.2000, the Government created a 'Task Force'– a Committee comprising top experts and headed by Girish Chandra (Gary) Saxena – to look into and report on the intelligence apparatus. A meticulously researched report making a wide range of

recommendations on reforming the intelligence set-ups was submitted to the Government in 2001.

96 To meet the challenges and problems, it called for a massive upgrading of technical, imaging, signal, electronic counter-intelligence and economic intelligence capabilities, and a system-wide reform of conventional human-intelligence gathering. A fair part of the Report has remained classified. In the years that ensued, most of its recommendations remained unimplemented in the face of bureaucratic resistance and an unenthusiastic political leadership.

The intelligence set-ups –4

97 Let us now detail the intelligence set-ups that presently exist. At the top of the intelligence pyramid is the National Security Council of India which comprises: (1) the National Security Advisory Board; (2) the Strategic Policy Group; and (3) the Joint Intelligence Committee (JIC).[18] The last (JIC) has its own Secretariat that works under the Cabinet Secretariat and analyses intelligence data from: (1) the Intelligence Bureau (IB); (2) the Research & Analysis Wing (RAW); and (3) the Directorates of Military, Naval and Air Intelligence.

98 Created originally in 1885, and re-cast in 1947, the Intelligence Bureau (under the Ministry of Home Affairs) is the premier internal intelligence organisation. Intelligence operations within the country are carried out by the Intelligence Bureau (IB) and its wide network of officers and men. The Intelligence Bureau maintains an array of branches and field units. All State Intelligence Bureaus are branches of their respective State police forces. And while their chiefs are supposed to be chosen in consultation with the IB chief, they mostly end up being political nominations.

99 The collection mechanisms of the Intelligence Bureau change depending on the focus, but the Intelligence Bureau executes its functions both at the National level and the State level. Employees of the Intelligence Bureau carry out the bulk of the intelligence collection strictly internally and only the senior officers generally undertake coordination and higher level management. The Intelligence Bureau functions in three main categories, namely, general, technical and ministerial.

100 Carved out of the Intelligence Bureau in 1968 to exclusively look after external intelligence is the Research and Analysis Wing (RAW) and its affiliated operational groups such as the Aviation Research Centre. It (RAW) collects and analyses external intelligence – pertaining to 'outside' India. It also reports to the National Security Adviser. Thus, external intelligence is the responsibility of the Research and Analysis Wing (RAW), working directly under the Cabinet Secretary, but reporting to the NSA for all practical purposes. RAW also keeps an eye on the activities of terrorist groups with bases in foreign countries. It has a

18 The Joint Intelligence Committee, which was merged with the National Security Council Secretariat in 1999, was revived in 2006.

vast budget, the extent of which is unknown; in fact, most available information about the RAW is largely speculative.

101 The next set of intelligence agencies are the military ones, led by the Directorate General of Military Intelligence (DGMI) with a network of field offices and forward posts in the border areas as well as representatives in diplomatic missions. Since the DGMI has historically been part of the Army, the Air Force and the Navy have individual intelligence units collecting and collating information relevant to their operations and bases. In 2002, the Defence Intelligence Agency (DIA) was created and entrusted with the task of coordinating the whole spectrum of military intelligence.

102 Apart from the Intelligence Bureau and RAW as the main Central agencies (and the military intelligence), the States also have their own Police LIUs, CID, Crime Branch, etc. Paramilitary forces like the Central Reserve Police Force and Border Security Force maintain their own intelligence units. So do the other government agencies providing physical security, like the Special Protection Group, National Security Guards and the Central Industrial Security Force.

103 As a sequel to the Saxena Committee Report and in order to optimise intelligence flow and co-ordination between multifarious agencies at the Centre and in the States in the field of counter-terrorism and counter-intelligence, the Central Government, in 2001, created a Multi-Agency Centre (MAC) and Joint Task Force on Intelligence (JTFI) in the Intelligence Bureau at Delhi, supported by Subsidiary Multi-Agency Centres (SMACs) in several State capitals.

104 The former was designed as the nodal centre for collating and analysing all internal security-related intelligence. The mission objective was to run an umbrella organisation comprising State-level units called SMACs and the development of a national counter-terrorism database supported by State-level police-intelligence Joint Task Forces and inter-State Intelligence Support Teams. The computing capabilities of the MAC would allow it to store not only the vast amount of information that flows in from the various agencies, but also inputs from State police forces.

105 Progress was delayed due to unseemly bureaucratic wrangling. Infighting among various intelligence agencies has affected its efficiency. Simply, the MAC has not been able to achieve its objectives. The MAC database now being planned would be capable of not just executing simple search operations, but also carrying out complex analytical operations.

106 Set up in 2004, as the repository of the nation's technical intelligence (TECHINT) capabilities to supply the security agencies and armed forces with technical intelligence, was the NTRO – National Technical Research Organisation. Like RAW, NTRO forms part of the Cabinet Secretariat and reports directly to National Security Adviser. The Chairman NTRO (also called Secretary) holds the same rank as the RAW chief.

107 NTRO, a highly specialised technical intelligence gathering agency, was envisaged to act as a super-feeder agency for providing technical intelligence to other agencies on internal and external security without affecting the working of the technical wings of the intelligence agencies, including those of the armed forces. Capability at cyber intelligence and cyber counter-intelligence; investigating cyber crimes; and cyber forensics and other cyber related services, including that of the protection of Government databases, was also envisaged.

108 With different government agencies protecting their turf in respect of intelligence gathering, NTRO is still to achieve its objectives. More than an organisation, as a concept, NTRO holds great promise. Only, we have to make the best out of it. Further description of the agencies as they stood in November 2008 is not necessary.

Some thoughts and views –5

109 Proceeding then to address a few more issues on intelligence, the system needs to be upgraded at the human, technical and operational levels. The reach has to be wide. Take, for instance, the traditional postman. He has a fair idea of who is who and, therefore, can be a useful source to the intelligence agencies for any suspicious activity.[19] However, with the mobile telephone and internet revolution, his role is declining, and this calls for making available a database of mobile telephone users, the call listings, and the location of the use, with the central agency so that for the basics, they do not have to run to the service provider. Something similar will have to be carved out for Internet usage. Attention towards counter-intelligence is also required.

110 The local intelligence unit of the regular (State) police (see para~ of Topic 11), which is not receiving the kind of support and attention as it should, requires a review to cope with terrorism. Here, however, a system of one-way communication to the central agency, which can refer back only in case of need (and sparingly), will be ideal. The same would also apply to the SHO of every police station in the country.

111 Another issue, easier said than covered by law, relates to employing officers and personnel with the intelligence agencies. The existing skill-deficit is compounded by several factors. The job requires a painstaking slog in anonymity and lacks the 'perks' that personnel posted with a 'lucrative' police station enjoy. It is only considered as 'punishment work' by most operatives. State-level special branches that gather intelligence are generally staffed with the dissatisfied lot. Most prefer to don the khaki uniform than be lost in stress-laden intelligence gathering jobs. Lack of motivation to join the intelligence agencies is also to be blamed on favouritism within the set-up, with upright officers being given short shrift and only a select few being promoted. The best of the talent available with the police forces, not wanting such a secondment, refuses to move to the intelligence agencies, thereby posing a series of long-term problems.

19 A similar obligation will also have to be placed on the courier agencies.

112 Another unfortunate part is that the intelligence organisations are mostly manned by administrators. The data collection process invariably takes place at some of the lowest rungs whereas the analysis, collation and archiving takes place at the middle rung. The field of intelligence requires officers and operatives to be given cover jobs, often at low levels, in order to carry out and achieve their task. There is, in practice, less than optimal focus on field operations and desk analysis operation activities. A constant 'check' on our own men is also required.

113 In order to improve the performance of the intelligence agencies, it is essential to enhance the quality of the people entering it. Instead of diverting people from the police or inducting recommendees of politicians and bureaucrats, intelligence requires talent-spotting at universities and at other levels.[20] The bright ones, whether for field work or for analysis on the computer, can be given short term commissions, renewable on performance.

114 The operative field staff – the people who actually conduct intelligence collection on ground – need far better terms of service. Incentives are required at every level to motivate officials to do their best. Individual calibre deserves greater consideration. Even otherwise, motivation has to be ensured. To fight the battle against terror, the immediate concern, therefore, is man-management – create the right intelligence team, upgrade its personnel profile and also insulate the set-up from any political interference.

115 Despite the fact that intelligence-gathering is a specialised skill, it has never been recognised as such. It needs a branch devoted to training ground-level personnel in intelligence-gathering techniques. The body of intelligence analysts must also be made responsible for continuously developing future incumbents, both in terms of ability as well as experience and expertise. Retired intelligence officials, including field operatives, need to be retained on the rolls for the purpose of training the younger generations in gathering grass-roots information, human intelligence operations, other covert operations, and technical analysis.

116 The promise to those who venture as field operatives and moles, or undertake other risky assignments, has to be backed by honouring the pledges given for such work. The credibility of the State on this score is at an all-time low. In the final analysis, the problem is both political and intra-bureaucracy rivalry. All these, however, are issues for the Government of the day to take care of, and cannot be part of law-making on this score.

The Role of Citizens –6

117 While the intelligence agencies will do their task, the fight against terrorism implies a duty on the part of the citizens – partly voluntary

20 The West has instances where convicts who were termed by the police and public prosecutors as 'super sharp minds' were offered tasks as operatives (spies) and those who agreed were, for record purposes, shown as killed in a prison fight or escaped from prison, and given new identities for the job.

and partly statutory.[21] It is obligatory to: (1) report suspicious activity (general duty); and (2) comply with the directions issued by the agencies (statutory duty). This is at the pre-event level. Once an incident has occurred and investigations are in progress, the duty takes a different form where such information as is available – which usually includes information of something in the past which was not considered relevant then, but, in the light of the subsequent incident, is found to be now relevant – must be communicated to the agency.

118 Both these duties will need a 'window' to which a citizen (the informant) can go with the confidence that: (1) there will at least be cognizance and consideration / examination; and (2) he himself will not be harassed.[22] Credibility of the Government in not disclosing the source or identity of the informant (so as to not expose him to risks) has to be sacrosanct.

119 A typical citizen can become the largest intelligence gathering source if that, as a source, is facilitated and encouraged. Putting in place various modes for a citizen to provide information through the right channel, verification of that information, secrecy of the identity of the informant, and other systems and safeguards, can provide us with the power to integrate information to make a meaningful intelligence report.

After 26/11 –7

120 On 26.11.2008, there was a terrorist attack on Mumbai. It came to be said that but for the failure of intelligence – particularly processing, taking note and then action – it would not have occurred. In an effort to improve national security, the Government got moving both on the intelligence front as also on setting up the National Investigation Agency and framing anti-terrorism law. The first part is addressed here and the second part (investigation agency and the stringent law) is addressed in sub-topic 8.

121 A number of measures were announced to effectively operationalise the institutional mechanism for intelligence collection, analysis, sharing and coordination with the State Governments viz. Multi-Agency Centre, Subsidiary Multi-Agency Centres, Joint Task Force on Intelligence and Inter-State Intelligence Support. An executive Order was issued by which the MAC has been obliged to share intelligence with all other intelligence agencies, including agencies of the State Governments. Likewise, all other agencies have been obligated to share intelligence with the MAC.

122 The Multi-Agency Centre (MAC), which is meant to collate intelligence inputs, assess them and disseminate its reports to the concerned agencies, is expected to now function round the clock as a central hotline for intelligence. SMACs, which so far exist in five State capitals, will also be established in the remaining State capitals. The States will need to set up round-the-clock control rooms under a Police officer of senior

21 See para~ of Topic 11 where a statutory obligation of citizens 'in know' to give information or even file a return has been mooted.

22 The second will not apply if he is deliberately giving false information in order to mislead.

superintendent level to share intelligence inputs on terrorism on a real-time basis with the MAC. With centralised command and control, a lead in, say, Uttar Pradesh, could help forestall an incident in Gujarat.

123 While 'sharing' information sounds good, it may, however, be noted that except for the database of individual information or other select information, to open or give access to all the databases to every intelligence agency is fraught with dangers.[23] Some data ought to be 'shared' and some not. A dividing line will have to be drawn. Criticism for lack of co-ordination among different agencies and reluctance to share information should not allow a pendulum swing to create a new set of problems where the terrorists know (through some of those who have access to the database) which of their movements or activities are being monitored by the intelligence agency, and therefore information sources are compromised and run dry. In practical terms, it may be necessary for a select few to do job work on a query for them rather than giving each the access to the whole database.

124 There is a massive drive to recruit field operatives where ex-servicemen are preferred. Then there are men who have been asked to operate under the cover of their private jobs. Also, capable officers and men are being sourced from the police, armed forces and paramilitary organisations for human, electronic and technical surveillance. The 'new terrorism' is demanding a revamped intelligence apparatus at the national level and a reinforced co-operation mechanism at the regional and local levels.

125 The process of augmenting and strengthening our counter-terrorism forces has also begun, and so has the process of strengthening maritime security against asymmetric threats from the sea. Coordinated measures to plug loopholes in regard to our air space are under way. To effectively implement and use geospatial technology for targeted counter-terrorism operations, legislation on that score needs a re-look so as to give it more clarity as also utility, if need be, by toning down existing restrictions. With access to such technology, it is possible to identify every vessel that enters our waters, making our coastlines that much more secure.

126 Closer scrutiny and attention as well as a more rapid response to new and emerging threats is required. The aim is to achieve the concept of total security, and this calls for deploying techniques such as structured analytic methodologies to convert the mass of information into actionable intelligence. It must be remembered that intelligence gathering involves: (1) Propensity tracking; (2) Opportunity tracking; (3) Logistical tracking; (4) Wherewithal tracking; and (5) Target identification and bulwarking.

127 Harking back, to the 2001 Report by a Committee comprising such stalwarts, in a work like this, nothing can be added in terms of thoughts for improvement. However, a few aspects, more from the common man's

---

23 Placing all information at one place has its advantages as also risks – of leaks or the source getting exposed.

point of view, may be highlighted. The broader objective is that he (the common man) understands the importance and nature of the task, the perils, the difficulties, and also the importance of letting those doing their task do that task without unnecessary criticism or fault-finding. More importantly, he has to: (1) recognise his own duty as a citizen; (2) tolerate intrusion into his privacy; and (3) pay lesser heed to self-professed critics[24] – for without such understanding by the public, as also support from it, the task of the intelligence and security set-ups becomes difficult.

Other matters, Issues and Tasks –8

128 There are some other matters, issues and tasks, reference to which may be made here for the sake of completeness. To begin, unlike the investigation agency, much, in fact most, of the intelligence apparatus will be faceless or secret. Systems and layers will need to be built, so that only the visible part thereof interacts with the National Investigation Agency, the regular (State) police, other government agencies, and the public. The details of the undercover officers and field operatives, and even analysts, just cannot be divulged. Data protection will be another formidable task. To preserve its functioning, it will have to be kept outside the purview of courts. The Media too will have to refrain from covering the former in any way.

129 The counter-terrorism agency would also require a secret Special Operations force to carry out covert operations. This might involve hot-pursuit or a strike at the terrorists' bases or hideouts. To leak or publish details of any such action (whether true or not) will have to be defined as a separate offence; even for what is factually an operation carried out by the unit, we, as a nation, will have to maintain a denial.

130 Another front that will require attention is terrorists' finances. Most terrorism financing in India occurs through informal channels, particularly *hawala*. The sleeper cells, which are often funded with fake currency, have developed an effective mechanism to escape the attention of intelligence agencies. They become active at will. There is also need to keep a strict vigil on all inflows and outflows of foreign and inland funds through the banking channels, or otherwise to detect any funds received ostensibly for legitimate purposes, but actually being diverted to terrorist organisations or individuals.

131 On this, there are, amongst others, the Central Economic Intelligence Bureau, Directorate of Revenue Intelligence, Enforcement Directorate[25]

24 some of whom may really be working at the instance of an enemy

25 The Central Economic Intelligence Bureau was set up in July, 1985 with the main objective of co-ordinating and strengthening the intelligence gathering activities, investigative efforts and enforcement action by the various agencies concerned with enforcement of economic laws. The Enforcement Directorate's functions are to collect and develop intelligence relating to violation of the provisions of Foreign Exchange Management Act and Prevention of Money Laundering Act 2002, conduct searches of suspected persons, and inquire into and investigate suspected financial transactions.

and Narcotics Control Bureau. In March 2006, a Financial Intelligence Unit (FIU) has also been set up. In carrying out their tasks, information of moneys or activities which could be related to terrorism is often to be found, and this must be relayed to the concerned anti-terrorism agency. In this regard and in so far as basic economic intelligence gathering is concerned, there is need for having a national database which could be used by all concerned agencies. A comprehensive Tax Information Network (TIN) is under way. See Topic 7~ of Chapter 9 at pp2~.

132 The discussion in Topic 5 (Money laundering) will also apply, but when it comes to following the terrorist's money trail, it will need further strengthening by way of Rules and Directions for record-keeping and reporting. However, a distinction between terrorism-related and other suspicious moneys has always to be maintained so that the former is pursued to the full degree while the latter is pursued only to the appropriate degree. Law should enable the economic resources of those suspected of terrorism to be attached and frozen, pending enquiry and investigation. Once again, the systems developed by some of the Western countries in the last few years can be studied and suitably adapted to situations and conditions in our country.

133 A word of caution. Information collected specifically in the name of preventing terrorism ought not to be made available for lesser wrongs like revenue evasion or even corruption. Unless such a distinction is maintained and a 'promise' to not use the information for any proceedings other than those under anti-terrorism laws is honoured, public cooperation and support may not be forthcoming. At the same time, whether it is the Intelligence Bureau or other financial intelligence gathering arms, we cannot allow their use for settling political scores or simply harassing citizens. Drawing the line between where to operate and where to stop may be difficult, but is a necessary task.

134 The intelligence set-ups as herein discussed will not only deal with issues relating to terrorism, but will also attend (either themselves or through separate but coordinated set-ups) to other problems such as: drugs & narcotics; organised crime, economic crime, etc., and crime control generally. To achieve efficiencies, each must specialise in a particular field, but any information that it come across, which may have a bearing on terrorist activity, must be passed on to the anti-terrorist cell.

135 Once again, the design and operational mechanics of the intelligence set-ups has to be left to the specialists in the field, only that the public (and the critics) have to leave them alone to do their task and cooperate when called for. More importantly, the public has to understand that unnecessary questioning on these matters, or even 'news' relating to intelligence operations, makes the task of national security difficult. At the same time, integrity of the officials, as also of the executive in control, to use these for the intended purpose and no other, is essential.

136 Discussion on intelligence has been placed here in Topic 10, and in some detail, because when it comes to protecting ourselves from terrorism, it is far more, in fact, most important. Going further into these issues will be beyond the scope of this work and suffice it is to lay emphasis on: (1) the importance of intelligence-gathering and processing; and (2) the need to look at it as separate from the investigation agency, which is for post-event.

General Policing, Anti-Terrorism Force and Crisis Management –9

137 We then come to what may broadly be called, policing and preventive. Policing is addressed in Topic 11. Three short points here: (1) improve the training and integrity of the typical policeman; (2) increase the police-population ratio; and (3) bring about the much awaited Police reforms.

138 A typical police constable may be unfit to fight a terrorist hand to hand, but in the fight against terrorism, the first place, naturally, goes to him. The basic eyes and ears (information to the concerned agencies), and the instant on the spot reaction will be provided by the general police. It is only on receiving inputs from the intelligence agencies or upon the actual happening of an event that the special task/security force would take over.

139 In other words, while the paramilitary or the NSG may assist the State administration in handling terrorist attacks, it is primarily the responsibility of the civil police to counter it at the first instance. But unfortunately, the police, in its present form and shape, is severely handicapped in dealing with the trained and highly committed bands of terrorists.

140 To think that every policeman is (or can be) proficient enough to fight a terrorist is a myth. It needs specially trained officers and commandos carrying sophisticated weapons and equipment to do so. However, what is required is better training of the typical policeman together with training on how to keep his eyes & ears open, inform the control post and control the situation till reinforcements arrive. To qualify for the task, fitness and regular training is essential, as is keeping the reflexes tuned.[26]

141 Law & Order being a State subject, and before we turn to the NSG, it is necessary that in every State, in fact in every district, an Anti-Terrorism Force (or more of a special task or security force) is established as part of the State Police. Hereinafter referred to as the (State's) StSG,[27] it will be a simpler version of the NSG. Located at strategic places in the State, it shall comprise personnel equipped with modern weapons and protective gear, and duly trained to take on any situation, including hostage rescue. A Rescue Team comprising fire-fighters, engineers, doctors, paramedics, ambulances, etc. is required as a companion set-up.

---

26 Regular firing practice, particularly of the *'all of a sudden'* (surprise) variety, is essential. A 12-year-old who regularly plays videogames (shooting a moving target) will be far quicker and accurate with a small firearm than a typical policeman with his ·303. On the harmful effect of such games, see sub-topic 6 of Topic 19 infra.

27 as an acronym for State Security Guards —a special unit of the State police

142 In the event of an attack, the StSG can rush to the crime scene with minimal response time – more like a fire brigade – with investigators and forensic experts in the tow, and proceed to take charge of the situation. Serving as a quick reaction team, it shall be far more effective as compared to the personnel at a typical police station. If the situation is so serious that it may not be possible for the StSG to handle, and it needs more, it is only then that the NSG be sent for.

143 In other words, the State Police will need to have its own Anti-Terrorism Security Guards – or the StSG as a paramilitary force on the lines of NSG – so that for terrorism-related matters, where there is no need to send for the NSG, this force can do the needful. The StSG's work, as also that of the rescue set-ups, will not be confined to terrorist acts, but they will be called for any operation, say, an accident, a natural disaster, or any other event requiring such services. A Crisis Management Group (at the State level) that combines the State administration along with the district and the local administration, and ensures quick decision-making and proper command control, is also required.

144 Moving then to the Centre, the National Security Guard (NSG) was set up in 1984 as a Federal Contingency Deployment Force, to handle anti-hijack operations, VIP security, rescue operations, and to provide tough support to the central para military forces in dealing with anti-terrorism activities in exceptional situations. The NSG is different from the Special Protection Group,[28] which is for the protection of the VVIPs.

145 Modelled on the pattern of the SAS of the UK and GSG-9 of Germany, the NSG is a task-oriented Force and has two complementary elements in the form of the Special Action Group (SAG), comprising Army personnel, and the Special Ranger Groups (SRG), comprising personnel drawn from the central para military forces / State police force. The training of the State Police personnel in anti-terrorism is also a part of its task. The very high level of training or 'standards' makes it necessary that NSG is sent for (used) only in exceptional situations.

146 After 26/11, where the NSG did a good job, expansion of the NSG as also setting up of four regional centres – in Mumbai, Kolkata, Chennai and Hyderabad – is under way. It is also proposed to set up NSG centres in more cities to facilitate quicker deployment. Such units are proposed to be located near the airports. The objective is that in case of a terrorist attack, an NSG commando unit should be able to reach any site in the country within a few hours until which time the local unit holds the fort. A coastal command is also being set up. More institutions for imparting training in counter-insurgency and commando operations are also planned.

147 There is also a school of thought which says that NSG be split into two

28 constituted under the Special Protection Group Act [34 of 1988] and modelled on the lines of the US Secret Service

separate bodies – one for the VIPs and the other for the general public. These are, however, matters for the experts to consider and decide.

148 The next step is the setting up of a permanent Crisis Management Group at the Centre to handle the fallout of major terrorist attacks anywhere in the country. While there are well-thought-out post-crisis management plans for earth-quakes, droughts and tsunamis,[29] there is none to handle a terrorist incident of the magnitude which Mumbai had witnessed.

149 There must be no ambiguity or confusion about who is in charge; Who will have overall authority over the different forces; Who will deploy the forces according to the needs of the situation; and Who will be held accountable for the success of the operation. Politicians, police chiefs and others at site – many, more eager to go live on television channels – is not crisis management. In the event of a terror attack, a proper command structure – with full powers at their disposal, and one that acts quickly and decisively – must be in place. Given the situation, we could even think of a virtual operations centre.

Equipping and protecting the Police and the Task Force –10

150 After the Mumbai episode, there has been public criticism of the State for leaving the police with ·303 bolt-action rifles of World War-1 vintage.[30] The public wants the Police to be armed with AK-47s, but doing so would be wrong. To handle an AK-47, it needs both training and responsibility. A typical policeman is not fit enough, and giving each one an AK-47 will only cause more problems. However, the ·303s need to be replaced by modern small firearms and other non-lethal incapacitating weapons as also electronics which auto-alert the central control room for reinforcement.

151 Unlike the past when the terrorists used crude weapons, the future will see sophisticated and state-of-the-art weaponry, together with ingenuous tactics. Whether it is a typical police constable, a senior police officer of the regular (State) police or a commando of the task force, they all need to be adequately equipped. While the regular police needs the basics, the assault forces (the NSG and the StSG) need to be equipped with special arms, light & effective weapons, incapacitating weapons & chemicals, night-vision / laser viewfinders, communication links to command control, and the like, as also protective gear such as bullet-proof jackets, ballistic-shields, helmets, etc.

152 There is no dearth of sophisticated equipment in the world market, but apart from the cost, the more important question to be addressed is: How should we go about it? Should we simply import it or develop our own?

---

29 The government has set up a National Crisis Management Committee and a Crisis Management Group. There is also a National Committee on Disaster Management to suggest the institutional and legislative measures necessary to manage natural disasters at the national, state and district levels.

30 This is not correct because in many places they have been issued self-loading rifles.

We have vast proven capabilities in the technological field. Instead of buying expensive off-the-shelf equipment from abroad, given the right environment, incentive and funds, such equipment is best developed in the IITs and then manufactured in our factories. It is the 'expertise' that is most important and this does not come without a hands-on approach. It is this which enables development of new technologies. Continuous research and development, and by our own people, is simply a must.

153 We must keep the latest and the best under wraps (while we continue our R&D for something 'still better'), provide the anti-terrorism outfits with the next rung, and release a version that is two rungs still lower to the general police. The battle is such that it will require constant thinking and attention. Bureaucratic delays and politico-executive indecision cannot be allowed to create impediments in development of technology.

154 The research and development will be on several other fronts as well; for example, techniques of data processing; information collating; automatic sweeps & scan over a mine of data to 'pick-up' the relevant; developing software for pattern-recognition and speech recognition; automatically searching for clues, and the like. There is need to develop systems for cracking codes & passwords (decoding), deciphering messages, decrypting, and the like, for interception of terrorist communication networks is an increasingly challenging task. Many of our youngsters have successfully developed software, hacked computer networks and carried out decryption. A high component of trial & error is however involved. They need to be given the opportunity to train, and then be employed for such tasks.

155 The problem of terrorism being what it is, it calls for greater reliance on these where, for several reasons, a system of keeping the latest equipment, technology as also methodology along with the brighter officers reserved for anti-terrorism activities and other important tasks, is necessary. The latest in technology and techniques needs to be kept as classified. Development of police technology, skills at investigation, and forensic sciences have been addressed in sub-topics 14, 15 and 16 of Topic 19 infra.

156 Stated simply, for research & development of technology – be it equipment or computer software – greater hope (and not scepticism) has to be placed in our boys and girls. They have to be given the opportunity of specialised education and training. Facilities for research & development be given to them and impediments removed. While success must be lauded, at times, failures also need a consolation prize. This is the human capital – rather the intellectual capital – that we need to build, which will then manifest itself as our technological might, hopefully, as a superpower. In any case, in the years to come, this alone can protect us as a nation.

157 The 'protection' required by the forces (and the police) is not only physical – against the terrorists' bullets and bombs – but also from legal issues. By the very nature of the task (which calls for split-second decision-

making), it sometimes happens that the police force by either error of judgment or deliberately planted information, or for other reasons – some explicable, some not – transgresses the bounds of reasonable and is accused of violating human rights. This completely demoralises the force. The resultant 'play safe' approach gives the terrorists an edge.

A National Identification System –11

158 Continuing with the measures that we need to adopt, the next is a national database of citizen information – or simply, a National Identification System – which in this age of information technology is not at all difficult to set up. On this score, one sensitive area is the illegal immigration into the country, which is increasingly difficult to track and control. Reports indicate that foreign terror groups find easy recruits amongst illegal immigrants, who are always looking for petty jobs, have no records or fixed place of abode, and have no emotional links with India. It is claimed by some that the local vote bank politics is the stifling factor, but that issue is being left aside here. In any case, national interest demands that an identification system with details of every citizen is put in place at the earliest. See Topic 19.9 infra.

Safety Measures –12

159 Prevention is better than cure. The 'intelligence' gathering discussed so far is mostly the duty of the State, but 'taking care' by every citizen is also necessary. While even general crime needs an element of attention towards its prevention rather than simply punishment of the guilty, with terrorism, this factor acquires greater importance. In all our activities and in all our locations, building in preventive and safety measures will reduce vulnerability or simply, the chances of success for a terrorist. Perhaps because of its low visibility, its utility has not been appreciated and sufficient attention has not been paid.

160 To be able to put in place safety measures, once again, we must address the psychology, and the thought process, of the terrorists. The terrorist here means not just the frontliner, but the one at the top as also the complete command chain which 'chooses' the target, develops the strategy, maybe carries out dry runs, and then strikes. It is analysing the thought process – no different than that addressed in sub-topic 3 of Topic 6 supra, but in a different form. The following are the other factors that those in command of a terrorist organisation usually take into consideration:

1 the ease with which injury to innocents can be caused, the extent of the injury, and the effect on the public and the government of such injury;

2 the probability of the frontliners and the logistic support team leaving evidence of their journey to the intended spot;

3 the chances of the frontliners being intercepted and thwarted;

4 the probabilities of the frontliners getting away (escape) vis-à-vis being captured alive, particularly whether they can divulge details

and lead back to the others involved directly and even those who are giving tacit support;

and the like. In a way, it is an assessment of the probabilities of such 'success' which they carry out, and with precision.

161 The importance of installing a wide network of surveillance cameras (CCTVs) cannot be overstated. CCTV cameras have not only to be many in number and strategically located, but also have to be functional, which requires regular checks. Installation of CCTVs in public places will reduce their vulnerability. Modern video surveillance cameras give very sharp images which are recorded as digital files on a hard disk and thus enable very low cost retention of files, and for long. The goal is a networked system of 'smart' video cameras that will let surveillance officers observe a wide area quickly and efficiently. Further, data has to be processed continually for suspicious activities and not just 'after' an incident. Computers will bear much of the workload. Systems as these will cause a shift in the thought process of the terrorists.

162 The availability of mobile telephony simcards and access to the Internet has also to be better controlled and monitored than at present. If a comprehensive application form with clearer photograph and more biometric details is received – and processed at the service provider (or at a State unit on the request of the service provider) – and the phone made functional only after clearance, things would be different. Likewise, for foreign simcards, filling-in of a similar form and verification can be made a pre-requisite before it becomes operational.

163 Preventive safety will take many forms and shapes, be it advance intimation of the travellers, frisking or luggage check, or quick processing of information before a person boards or alights. The public transportation systems, airlines and railways will need to cooperate with the central intelligence agencies. Like this, there will be a host of measures.

164 Town planning, municipal and structural mapping and record-keeping; and finally, training beat constables, may seem trivial and unconnected measures when dealing with terror, but can eventually make a big difference. The unbridled growth of slums and unauthorised colonies have offered ready habitats to the terrorists and considerably blunted the police effort to trace them.

165 We also need to have a separate department under the Home Ministry (which in turn interacts with the MAC) to issue alerts and warnings based on intelligence inputs. Such alerts and warnings will have to be not at a 'high' all the time, but will need to be more specific and accurately graded. Many will need to be communicated only to one or two persons of the suspect target organisation, rather than have them reported in the press.

166 Another Body can be set up to carry out vulnerability assessments and give advice on preventive / safety measures to those who request for it.

A professional advisory service as this must be made available by the State for a price to the business, industrial and institutional sector.

167 The security of the citizens is the responsibility of the State (executive), but the limitation of the executive on this count (i.e. to protect the citizens) must be recognised. While every citizen will also have to contribute to the effort (so as to reduce risks and vulnerability), with the Indian economy growing, a special problem arises with regard to the Industries, Corporates, Special Educational Institutions, Shopping Malls, Hotels, Banks, etc. – or simply, INDIA-INC.

168 The private security arrangements and services for them have their limitations as to the training, quality, equipment, and more particularly, the firearms licences. The last must be more than mere ceremonial display. There are also ramifications of their actual use, which need laws that conform to realities. The requirement being imperative, and huge, it needs a joint venture – a public-private partnership – to look after various aspects, from training to equipment and finally, to enabling (and protecting) laws and rules. Only to depict the magnitude, even the screening of employ--ees with the help of State machinery may be necessary in some cases.

169 Another issue, generally overlooked, is that the security personnel need to be directed towards preventive measures by capability at quick reaction rather than having a ceremonial presence in important or busy places. A few trained men (in plain clothes) can, as a quick reaction team, far better deal with any threatening situation till reinforcements arrive. Similarly, trained persons (secretly armed) can be deployed as ordinary employees in the establishments in busy places or left to run petty stalls.

170 Safety and taking care are the watchwords. The design – or the How to ensure safety – has to emanate from a central set-up, but in the ultimate, it is the citizens who have to take care, be alert and also put up with the slowdown, costs, and other nuisances of such safety measures.

Preventive Detention and other Controls –13

171 One tool in the hands of the Executive that deserves address here is of preventive detention. Often, the past activities, the intentions harboured, and other inclinations of a person clearly point to his involvement in terrorism, or there may be only strong suspicion. At other times, the information may be only about preparatory activities, or of 'parts', some of which may not be terrorism-related in entirety. However, all these may not be sufficient as proof to convict in a court of law,[31] in which case there is need to wield the jurisdiction of suspicion or preventive detention.

172 The AT-law needs to empower the Central and State Governments to order preventive detention of any person based on intelligence inputs. It will require a special statute and procedures in that regard. It will also need to provide that during preventive detention, if the detenu is tried and

31 based on intelligence reports, or a firm belief with the executive

acquitted, the earlier order of preventive detention would not automatic--ally lapse. However, it may be a ground for reconsidering the continuance of the detention. See also para 309 infra for enabling the Court to so order. Since the discussion on preventive detention in Topic 7 (sub-topic 8 at pp3~ supra) is detailed, further discussion is not necessary.

173 Alongside preventive detention, the Central / State Authority will also need to have powers to order Special restraints and / or direct Continued surveillance – S-Restraints and C-Surveillance for short. It will generally help reduce terrorist activity and may even help bring many acts, which are at best an 'attempt', within the net. The operational mechanics of these tools have been detailed in Topic 18. See also para 313 infra.

174 Another preventive measure is the banning of organisations notorious for directly or indirectly destabilising the government with ulterior motive or subverting the rule of law and economy of the country. However, of late, banning an organisation has come to mean little, for it is cohesion and conspiracy between those involved that matters and not the label (name) which they adopt for themselves as an entity. It is not a consumer product which will lose much of its sales upon being asked to change its name. In fact, the controversy regarding the banning and the continuous 'news' of it gives it the much-needed publicity, which then acts as a focal point for identity recognition.

Attending to the causes –14

175 Away from the realm of intelligence, policing, laws & procedures, when it comes to dealing with terrorism, social and economic measures also assume importance. Law alone cannot find a permanent solution to this menace. A terrorist is very different from a typical criminal and what drives him to take to terror may not always be wholly unjustified. To say that all these concerns can be swept under the carpet, in the name of peace, civil society and national safety, is wrong.

176 To find a solution to internal problems, the causative factors and the dissatisfaction amongst the masses of the region should be determined and remedied. We cannot wrongly give a label of 'terrorist' to those with a genuine cause – and more so where the democratic principles and systems of expression / communication avenues give (in practical terms) neither a proper hearing nor fetch the deserved response (action).

177 A genuine voice of a citizen, deserving hearing and attention, cannot be suppressed by simply terming it as 'terror'. It is the rule of law and democratic principles which need to be upheld. That apart, agrarian crisis, unemployment and lack of education enable self-professed revolutionaries to indoctrinate the minds of the gullible youth. In any case, unless an approach of listening and making every endeavour to attend to the justified component of the demand is made, the fight against terrorism will only find disaffection and discontent growing. We have also to counter the mischievous propaganda of terrorist groups.

178 The feasibility of organising education and information camps in the terrorism affected areas will also need to be explored. This will help break down the psychological support for terrorist activities and even public approval of them by a section of the populace. The breeding pools for these cadres have to be drained by providing far better delivery of public goods and services to the poorest. This requires better governance and greater accountability. Corruption in various spheres of governance, particularly daily life, drives some people to sympathise with terrorists and also makes it easy for them to find roots and fester without being detected.

179 Lastly, the fight against terror is such that it will require attention to very many more issues (and topics) than those noted here. In any case, tackling terror is a long-term project. It does not end with being tough on the stray one caught in the process. We have to nip terror in the bud – and also, preferably, prevent it from taking root.

8. The Offence, Trial and Punishment

180 No matter what preventive measures (as discussed so far) we may introduce, it will only increase the safety levels, but not eliminate all risks. There will still be occasions where there is breach – big or small – and to investigate, prosecute and punish such breaches, it will call for laws, investigators, prosecutors, courts, prisons and corrections. Law has to address these issues in an appropriate context, which is why (separate from establishing intelligence and other agencies) it calls for: (1) a substantive law that is different from the norm; (2) trial before special courts, which follow duly tailored procedures; (3) easy transfer to and from special courts to other courts; (4) degrees (classes) of guilt; and (5) innovative forms of punishment that are tailored to meet the objective.

181 There is also the need for putting in place all such systems, including statutory obligations of citizens which alter or affect the factors that either give easy passage and safe haven for the terrorists or make difficult the work of law enforcement agencies to nab them. This is one reason why it is said that laws against terrorism are not just about defining the offence, prescribing punishment and providing the adjudication procedures alone; it involves doing far more, the effect of which might not be openly visible, but would be very much there.

182 As noted in sub-topic 2 (paras 15 to 19) supra, after the 26/11 attack on Mumbai, by Act 35 of 2008 [31.12.2008], the Unlawful Activities (Prevention) Act [37 of 1967] has been further amended. The discussion here, however, does not address this particular statute, but addresses anti-terrorism law as a concept. Reference is made to some of the provisions as they exist, and many which do not exist, only as thoughts for consideration. A broader concept is put forward with the objective of being of some utility while developing and fine-tuning laws and procedures in this regard. This explains why some part of the discussion (on statutory provisions) may also run counter to the existing provisions.

183 It is for this reason that here, the statute is referred to as AT-law and not as 'UAPA'. Furthermore, the term AT-laws, depending on the context, will also include the laws chalking out the Dos and Don'ts for the general public, when such actions/omissions come to have a bearing on terrorism.

184 While intelligence agencies have been addressed in the last sub-topic, the investigation agencies (which are distinct therefrom) are addressed here – again as a concept and not as the newly created (by Act 34 of 2008) National Investigation Agency in particular, although reference to it as the NIA is, at times, made. A special anti-terrorism investigation agency of the State police (and as distinct from the SHO of the police station where the terrorist act took place) is also propounded for taking up matters which are not taken up by the NIA, or for investigation till the NIA takes over. This agency, again as a concept, is referred to here as the StIA.[32] In similar vein, on the lines of the NSG, the States will need to have their own Anti-Terrorism Security Guards (StSG). See para 141.

185 Insofar as the courts are concerned, TADA had used the term 'Designated Court', POTA had used 'Special Court', and MCOCA and the like statutes, all use the term 'Special Court'. Following the same trend, Chapter IV (Section 11) of the National Investigation Agency Act [34 of 2008] gives power to the Central Government to constitute special courts and provides for matters relating to the working of such courts.[33] Again for the reason that the discussion here deals with concepts and not specific statutes, this topic uses the term 'AT-Court'– a short form for a special court designated to take cognizance of offences under the anti-terrorism laws, and for their trial.

Defining the Offence and prescribing the Punishment–1

186 Section 15 of the Unlawful Activities (Prevention) Act, as amended, reads:

15. Whoever does any act with intent to threaten or likely to threaten the unity, integrity, security or sovereignty of India or with intent to strike terror or likely to strike terror in the people or any section of the people in India or in any foreign country:

(a) by using bombs, dynamite or other explosive substances or inflammable substances or firearms or other lethal weapons or poisonous or noxious gases or other chemicals or by any other substances (whether biological, radioactive, nuclear or otherwise) of a hazardous nature or by any other means of whatever nature to cause or likely to cause:

(i) death of, or injuries to, any person or persons; or

(ii) loss of, or damage to, or destruction of, property; or

(iii) disruption of any supplies or services essential to the life of the community in India or in any foreign country; or

---

32 as an acronym for the State's Anti-Terrorism Investigation Agency. Most of the States have their own anti-terrorism units of the police.

33 Perhaps, instead of being established under the Investigation Agency Act, the courts could have been established under a separate statute for the purpose.

(iv) damage or destruction of any property in India or in a foreign country used or intended to be used for the defence of India or in connection with any other purposes of the Government of India, any State Government or any of their agencies; or

(b) overawes by means of criminal force or the show of criminal force or attempts to do so or causes death of any public functionary or attempts to cause death of any public functionary; or

(c) detains, kidnaps or abducts any person and threatens to kill or injure such person or does any other act in order to compel the Government of India, any State Government or the Government of a foreign country or any other person to do or abstain from doing any act,

commits a terrorist act.

The amended (or new) Sections 16A, 17, 18, 18A, 18B, 23, 24, and 25 also contain provisions that further define the offences.

187 Proceeding then to address the issues, and more on principle, the term terrorism can be a nebulous concept, eluding a clear definition. Despite the attention being devoted to terrorism studies, there is no consensus on a fundamental question: How to define terrorism? Many have striven to find a definition. Conclusions and proposals have been diverse. The United States' Department of Defence defines terrorism as:

> The calculated use of unlawful violence or threat of unlawful violence to inculcate fear; intended to coerce or to intimidate governments or societies in the pursuit of goals that are generally political, religious, or ideological.

Within this definition, there are three key elements – violence, fear, and intimidation. Each element produces terror in its victims.

188 The US Dept. of State defines terrorism to be premeditated politically-motivated violence perpetrated against non-combatant targets by sub-national groups or clandestine agents, usually intended to influence an audience. Their FBI, too, has put forward a definition in these words: Terrorism is the unlawful use of force and violence against persons or property to intimidate or coerce a government, the civilian population, or any segment thereof, in furtherance of political or social objectives.

189 A component in the definition might include 'mass destruction'. Then, terrorism is not only bullets and bombs. In its recent manifestations, it can take many forms and modes – cyber attack on Government, institutional or business mainframe computer networks; pumping fake currency; or otherwise disrupting administration, to name a few.

190 Terrorism has within its ambit various activities which cannot be precisely described. It needs a wide definition. There are two parts here. The first is that an act (or omission) standing in isolation may be perfectly legal – even normal or routine. However, when many such acts (or omissions) combine together to become components of that which ultimately appears as a terrorist act, then that very act (or omission)

– otherwise lawful – becomes a wrong, which the society needs to punish in order to prevent the larger wrong (terrorism). The principle – at times called Gestalt – is that the whole can be, and often is, something which is different from its parts, and usually even larger than the sum of its parts.

191 Further, terrorism-related prosecutions and trials are not confined to that of the terrorist who was arrested at the time of the incident or soon thereafter (i.e. the visible one), but also include a host of others. Furthermore, the attempt may have failed or it may have been foiled; nevertheless there has been an offence, whether serious or borderline or even trivial. Therefore, terrorism, being what it is, will need attention, and a definition that covers each of the very many areas and roles, which vary from active and central to peripheral and insignificant, including those merely facilitating it or just encouraging it, or simply failing to take care.

192 Unlike most other crimes, terrorist activities are usually unearthed through intelligence (and even undercover) operations. This often leads, as it should, to the interception of terrorists virtually in their mid-tracks, at which point of time all the elements of a terrorist offence may not be complete. Dilemma of the enforcement agencies is: (1) exposure of the terrorists at this stage may prevent a terrorist strike, but since the offence or its preparation was not complete, it may not entail any effective legal action against the culprits; and (2) allowing them to proceed further[34] so as to book them later for their act carries a risk of their plan succeeding, which is why a wide definition is called for.

193 Some say that the definition of a terrorist act should not be that wide, but remain more restricted or narrow, and more so to prevent misuse. But unless the definition is wide, how do we book the various persons (or acts and omissions) or each of the components – like each of the many links of a long chain or pieces of a jigsaw puzzle – which enable the carrying out of the ultimate terrorist act, or even make it difficult to prevent? Mere preparation for a terrorist act can itself be an offence, as can proof of a failed attempt. A wide definition, with careful application, is necessary.

194 Two offences, well known to criminal jurisprudence, are: (1) abetment; and (2) conspiracy. To prove the charge of abetment, the prosecution is required to prove that the abettor had instigated the doing of a particular thing or engaged with one or more other person/s in any conspiracy for the doing of that thing or intentionally aided by an act of illegal omission, the doing of that thing. Conspiracy to commit an offence is itself an offence and a person can be separately charged with respect to such a conspiracy. There may be an element of abetment in a conspiracy; but conspiracy is something more than mere abetment.

34 Often, the terrorists will be allowed to work on their plan till it nears fruition, when the police / commando unit would swoop down on them.

195 Departing from traditional criminal law, for terrorism-related matters, two more provisions need to be added: (3) 'directly or indirectly facilitated the commission of the offence'; and (4) 'failed to take such care which, if it had been taken, would have prevented the commission of the offence'. The use of the word 'facilitate' (in 3) gives it a wider meaning than the word 'abet', where some element of positive intention flowing from the accused must inhere, but it is not necessarily so with the mere word 'facilitate'. Stated differently, while 'aid or abet' may mean 'facilitate', 'facilitate' does not necessarily mean 'aid or abet'. 'Facilitate' is wider in import and can take place even without intent.

196 The last of them (i.e., 4) imports the tort principle of 'reasonable care' and makes it very wide. This could involve a wholly innocent person, but in the fight against terrorism, that becomes a necessary evil. Breach of statutory obligations by otherwise law-abiding citizens, which has an unintended effect of aiding terrorism, will also have to be suitably covered. An example would be of a landlord not reporting a new tenant to the local police. Such 'care' would ordinarily be as 'Directions' as part of the Rules / notifications of the local administration, but even when absent, the breach can fall within the meaning of 'failing to take care'.

197 Innocent breach by a person but for which the terrorist would not have succeeded being defined as an offence is only a species of criminal negligence. An explanation would be required that whether the main offence (terror attack) was completed or stood aborted would have no bearing on this offence, for it is the breach of duty that is sought to be defined as an offence and made punishable. However, the punishment for this offence ought not to be stringent, and the courts too ought to be careful while sentencing.

198 Acts of commission or omission referred to above would include those without intent which prevented generation, capture, retention and preservation of evidence in relation to terrorist activity, or evidence as would help nab the terrorist. This would be a variant of the offence of destruction of evidence, but would cover both pre- and post-event acts, and also cover absence of *mens rea* on the part of the wrongdoer. However, the courts will take care not to overly punish for the 'absent mens rea' types of offences.

199 With terrorism, for practical considerations, it may be advisable that the definition be in two separate parts: (1) terrorist offence; and (2) terrorism-related offence. Terrorism and terrorism-related activities cannot be judged on the same ground. The former will cover those whose infractions are per se acts of terrorism (or as is the current definition of terrorism in some of the Western countries); the second will cover offences by those who are not otherwise involved in terrorism, but whose actions (or omissions) have the effect of facilitating or making it difficult to prevent terrorism.

200 The use of the Internet or other communication facilities for aiding terrorism should also be defined as an offence. So should assisting and financing terrorism. In fact, merely propagating terrorism is a wrong. Availability of weapons with the terrorists deserves special attention. Arms, explosives, and other weapons and devices used by terrorists – rather than being left to the statute against terrorism alone – are best further defined by a clarification in the Rules, the periodic framing of which the statute must provide for. Disseminating information that assists in the manufacture of such weapons could also be defined as an offence.

201 The purpose of ensuring that no terrorist act escapes the statutory definition can be achieved by treating any act or omission which leads to the defined result as a 'terrorist act'. And in that stray case where there arises a difficulty or doubt, the law must make an exception, for tackling terrorism, by making a provision that enables a clarificatory notification, which takes effect retrospectively. This is so because legislation, at times, does not keep pace with technology as also the methodology involved. In fact, in the fight against terrorism, an element of retrospective legislation – despite its ostensible clash with Article 20 (1) – must be explored.

202 While the definition must be wide – and as wide as possible – care must be taken by the police (investigators), prosecutors and courts, that the width is understood and applied in the context of the statute; or applied properly according to the purpose and not by a literal interpretation, the effect of which might run counter to the statute's intent. This is so because unless the definition is very wide, the real terrorist and those assisting him could escape, and conversely, if a full meaning to that wide definition is given, even a passenger in a bus, who sub-consciously responds to a *Namaste* from a stranger (who is a terrorist), could be (technically) accused of the offence of communicating with a terrorist.

203 Those responsible for enforcement (initially) and, thereafter, prosecution, and finally, the courts, will have to examine each particular case to see whether application of the wide definition is really called for. But as a basis for the statute, a wide definition is imperative.

204 Considering the volume of definitions which have been enunciated in various legislations worldwide over the last several years as also in numerous scholarly papers, it will not serve any purpose for this work to dwell further on that and we can rely on the extensive material that already exists.[35] Suffice it to note here that we as a nation ought to adopt a definition that comports with that in use in some of the Western nations, duly adapted to our conditions, and also takes into account the procedural, preventive and punitive tools that this work propounds.

---

35 See for instance: The Definition of Terrorism – A Report by Lord Carlile of Berriew Q.C. (as an Independent Reviewer of Terrorism Legislation) presented to the UK Parliament (March 2007).

205 The punishment for the various offences will have to be scientifically researched and then prescribed. Contrary to traditional criminal sentencing, it will, at the same time, establish a post-conviction Control Authority,[36] which can recommend the suspension of the sentence, or if there be resumption of any improper activity by the convict, revocation of the suspension. See para 298 *et seq.*

Companion and Related Laws - 2

206 The concept of tough laws to deal with terrorism ought not to be mixed up with the concept of laws (statutes) dealing with organised crime; public order; law & order; and the like. They are separate – of lesser levels of stringency – though there will need to be a sufficient overlap between them. Putting in place laws such as these is essential; otherwise the police tends to use the anti-terrorism laws against such offenders (maybe as a temporary remedy) and that is counterproductive.

207 To explain the strength (or stringency of laws), we can take the illustration of a simple hammer.[37] In weight, it can range from 10 grams on the underside[38] to 10 kg on the upper.[39] Now, in a mechanical workshop that has to attend to all kinds of tooling and job works, and in large numbers – quite like law has to attend to a wide variety of wrongs and offences that take place in society – to have non-availability of hammers in the range between 10 gms to 50 gms; a few between 50 gms to 100 gms; the bulk between 0.1 kg to 1 kg; next to nothing in the 2 kg to 7 kg range;[40] and then have a 10 kg one,[41] is wrong. It only defeats the purpose.

208 It is this gap – absence of laws, the stringency of which is equivalent to hammers in the range of 2 kg to 7 kg – which makes the system (police) use the anti-terrorism law in situations where the real need is for laws equivalent to a 2, 3, 5 or 7 kg hammer. No wonder that when a problem requiring a law having a stringency (potency) equivalent to a 10 kg hammer occurs, it is found that public criticism based on past misuse of the '10 kg' law has resulted in that having been removed from the inventory.

209 Another illustration could be of a physician / doctor prescribing – despite the side effects and other consequences – a high potency wide-spectrum antibiotic even for a minor or medium ailment, only because his kitbag (or the chemist shop) does not have medicines of the mid-potency range.

210 These illustrations were only about the weight, potency or strength. Equally important is the design, rather the 'tailoring', of the law, both

---

36 which, on the likes of a Probation Officer, needs to be established. Procedures to be followed by it, and by the State Government and Court will have to be developed and put in place.

37 as spanner sizes will not be adequately illustrative. The hammer described here is that used by a single person.

38 more like the ones with a jeweller or a precision engineer

39 like the one with a blacksmith at a foundry or those at truck repair shops

40 in which 'range' laws relating to Organised Crime, Public Order, etc. will fall

41 akin to the anti-terrorism law

substantive and procedural, so that – just like the specifically designed single-hex socket wrench with a long shank and robust lever can reach to and tackle even the most difficult nut, which a standard bi-hex open jaw spanner cannot, or the precise drug can which cure a particular ailment for which it is formulated while others cannot – carefully drafted and continually updated AT-laws can address terrorism in all its manifestations.

211 Apart from laws of intermediate stringency as aforesaid, there is need for law to provide the 'Dos and Don'ts' for the general public with a view to prevent terrorism. Such obligations, and in a clear form, will have to be placed not in the anti-terrorism statute, but in a number of other statutes / rules – be it as simple as the use of a vehicle, cell-phone simcard, Internet connection or bank account – to cover the entire spectrum.

Offence-Specific Tailoring of Procedures – 3

212 Moving from substantive law to procedural law, presently, the procedure as provided by the 1973 Code [2 of 1974] is followed for the trial of most of the offences, except where certain parts thereof are, by AT-laws, amended in their application to anti-terrorism prosecutions. That, however, is not enough, for the trial of offences under AT-laws needs special procedures that are tailored to the nature of the problem.

213 Topic 14 in general (and sub-topic 3 thereof in particular) points out how offence-specific tailoring of procedures can bring about greater accuracy, efficiency, as also speed, when it comes to criminal prosecutions / trials. The same principle would apply here. We need a companion procedural code that is tailored to the subject (terrorism). Some of the thoughts in the ensuing portion proceed on that basis, though in this discussion, and as a broad pattern, the structure of the 1973 Code has been adopted.

214 Further, laws on this score (both substantive and procedural) will need excellence in drafting with full reliance upon delegated legislation.[42] Continuous updating of the anti-terrorism laws being essential, input from experts will be of help. An official appendix (revisable by a notification) may enlist the Rules, notifications and other statutory provisions having a bearing on or relevance to the subject. Stated differently, a thorough analysis of a number of factors – input on many of which can be given by the intelligence and investigation agencies as also the prosecutors and Judges – will have to be constantly carried out for keeping the AT-laws fine-tuned.

Arrests and Bails – 4

215 Once information of a terrorist act is received, several tasks are to be carried out, the first of which is arrests.[43] To take into custody those suspected of having committed terrorist offences is no easy task. On the one hand, they could be so heavily armed that it is impossible to capture and arrest them, and on the other hand, they may appear simple and docile and be in the guise of a most law-abiding citizen. In these

---

42 See the discussion on these issues in Topic 2 of Chapter 9 supra.

43 See the discussion on 'arrests' by the police in Topic 11 infra.

circumstances, a police officer may find it difficult to believe that the particular person he is looking for is involved in terrorism. Further, in some regions, with the police in pursuit, the stance of the local population could also be anti-police, which would not be so if the police were looking out for a typical murderer or rapist. Consequently, in order to effect arrests, unconventional approaches may need to be adopted.

216 Then, upon arrest, the guidelines to the police issued by the Supreme Court in *D.K. Basu vs State of West Bengal*,[44] which spell out the rights of an arrestee in custody (to be followed in all cases of arrest or detention), particularly the warning contained in para 36 thereof, create an impediment when it comes to handling cases of terrorism. Presently, if a person is arrested in relation to a terrorist offence, and is being interrogated, there have been instances of human rights activists (usually accompanied by the media persons and even lawyers) crowding the interrogation centre and claiming a right to meet the arrested militant. With that as the scene outside, the arrestee is less likely to make disclosures nor can proper interrogation be carried out. This also alerts the others involved with him, making their arrest more difficult.

217 Here, it is to be remembered that most law-making involves striking a balance between competing demands and forces. With typical policing, when there is a tussle between the local SHO and the run-of-the-mill or hardened criminal (or even an innocent who has incurred the former's suspicion or wrath), these guidelines strike the right balance. But when it comes to terrorists or those suspected of being involved in terrorism, different considerations prevail. The 'guidelines' need a proviso (or an exception) that they would not apply if the arrest is for a terrorism-related offence. In any case, these guidelines (in *D.K. Basu*) are transitory till law in that regard is framed by the legislature.

218 Investigation commenced; arrest made; the next question is of forwarding (producing) the arrestee before the competent court.[45] For terrorism-related offences, the period of 24 hours needs to be extended to 48 hours; and further extendable to seven days, provided that within 36 hours of the arrest, the District Judge or the AT-Court has been informed.[46] A senior officer from the NIA or the StIA will have to certify that there is sufficient ground for exercise of the proposed exception to the rule. A provision as this is necessary so as to prevent the others involved from knowing that one of their comrades has been arrested.

219 A worrying factor at this point is the over enthusiasm shown by the media in highlighting the details of the arrest by the police and the investigations conducted by the investigating authority. Such publicity by the media does incalculable harm. The police, in turn, try and overcome this

---

44 1997-1 SCC 416 = AIR 1997 SC 610

45 See Section 167 Cr.P.C. See also Article 22(2) of the Constitution.

46 and who may be requested to keep the information secret

by keeping the arrest off the record, which again is not right. In such a scenario, silence by the police (or even a false denial before the media) ought not to counted as being contra as it is only to prevent making the comrades of the terrorist aware that one of their companions has been arrested and also to avoid any retaliatory action on their part.

220 For terrorism-related matters, the limit of 15 days in police custody needs to be extended (with permission of the court) to 30 days, with a further right to later (upon assigning reasons) take back to police custody from the judicial custody for period/s which do not exceed 45 days in total, including the time at the initial stage. Custodial interrogation becomes particularly necessary because others involved may have been arrested only later, or other information gathered at a later stage.[47]

221 Here, however, the statute must clarify that if an order of preventive detention is in force, that would not be affected. A longer period of detention without the formal charge sheet is necessary because time-consuming and painstaking investigations are required for such offences since those involved usually take every care to cover their tracks. Extensive data may have to be sifted through and processed. It involves much more than just finding out who all witnessed B murdering C in the central market, or a few other related matters.

222 Immediately upon arrest, and in any case after producing the accused before the Court, arises the question of bail. Bail has been addressed in detail in Topic 12 infra. Section 43D(4) to (7) of the UAPA attends to bail. In terrorism-related arrests, bail is difficult to come by. To make it that difficult to get bail and leave it to the police – by simply giving the label of a terrorist or terrorist-related – to take away, in practical terms, the right to bail, is not proper. Innocents, who get entangled, need some respite.

223 The correct approach would be that the statute may require the Court to: (1) be circumspect (although that term is nebulous); and (2) take recourse to innovative conditions (some of which are noted in Topic 12 infra).[48] The rest can develop as a matter of precedent and practice. However, where bail is to be granted, the grant of bail must, unless the Court specifically orders otherwise, take effect only after three days so as to enable an appeal / revision by the State. For compulsive bail (for non-filing of charge sheet), the UAPA rightly extends the period to 90 days, with a proviso which permits an extension up to 90 days (total 180 days).

224 Lastly, and unlike the traditional procedure for cancellation (see pp3~ infra), on filing the charge sheet, and upon taking cognizance, a provision for

47 Several provisions somewhat on the lines of the thoughts noted here have, only in relation to a case involving an offence punishable under UAPA, been inserted [31.12.2008] by the UAPA in Section 167 Cr.P.C.

48 See para~ in Topic 12 – Bails – at pp3~ supra. Topic 12 infra also argues a case for refusing bail to an accused who is otherwise entitled, on the ground that his release will endanger the safety of the community.

automatic cancellation of Bail and its reconsideration (re-grant / refusal) is essential. Further, another round of consideration of the Bail is called for at the stage of framing the charge, though as a matter of practice, the two stages could combine into one, i.e., the later one.

Investigation –5

225 Courts decide on the basis of the evidence collected by the investigation agency and presented by the prosecution, after weighing (evaluating) it against the presumption of innocence. The importance of comprehensive and fair investigations cannot be overstated. Investigation of crime is carried out by the officer-in-charge of a police station (SHO) within whose jurisdiction the offence was committed.[49] However, investigating a terrorist act (or activity) is quite different from investigating general crime, and can be complex. It is sometimes beyond the ken of a typical SHO.

226 After the 26/11 attack on Mumbai, the National Investigation Agency has been established under Act 35 of 2008 [31.12.2008]. The statute empowers the concerned police officials at the level of SHOs across the country to pass on information of a 'scheduled crime' to the NIA within 15 days of registration of a crime. If the NIA decides to take up the investigations, its officers will assume the investigation powers of the local police with regard to the concerned crime. The State Government shall extend all assistance to NIA for investigation of terrorism-related offences.

227 One difficulty will, however, be encountered in such a process. By the time the local police / State Government transfers the matter to NIA and they take charge, the elapse of time would be detrimental to the investigation. There could be loss of vital clues due to inadept handling of physical evidence. There can be disturbance of the crime scene, escape of the persons concerned, and other negatives. With criminal investigation, the earliest days, in fact hours, are most important. Therefore, a preferred system would be to establish a special anti-terrorism investigation agency in each State, or the StIA as referred to in para 184 supra.

228 Keeping in view the nature of the problem as also the general psychology and practicality, it is desirable that on reliable information of terrorist activity being received, the investigation is taken up by the State's Anti-Terrorism Investigation Agency (StIA)[50] and on preliminary or further investigation, if it turns out to be an ordinary crime, or the incident does not turn out to be terrorism-related, it can be left to the local SHO to take over and continue with the investigation. Conversely, if the SHO suspects that there is more to that than meets the eye, i.e., there is a semblance of terrorism, he may request the StIA to also have a look.

229 Put simply, when a fire is suspected, it is better to send the trained fire brigade with its ringing brass bells in time rather than take hours to decide whether to send for it, by which time much of the damage may be

49 For the powers of the police to investigate, see Chapter 12 of the 1973 Code.

50 The local police shall act under its command and assist this team as required.

beyond salvage. The fire brigade can always return to the fire station if the local fire extinguisher has succeeded in quelling the fire. The 'flow' has to be generally in this direction and only in rare cases where the SHO, during the investigation of some offence, finds terrorism-related features, that he can request the NIA or the StIA to have a look or even take over.

230 Whether it is the NIA, or the StIA, the investigators must be well trained, well equipped and keep themselves up to date with the current thought on investigating terrorism-related offences and the tactics of terrorists. Apart from training in investigation for such offences, they will also have greater means of communication for sending out queries to the home database seeking returns or interacting with the MAC or other investigation agencies to have matters in other places, towns, cities or even villages 'checked up'. They can effectively use LIUs of the State police at other places for any query, information or return as compared to what a typical SHO can do by himself. The same applies to forensic support services and turnaround time from the sophisticated laboratories.

231 The NIA/StIA will be a team which will include forensic and other experts. This will ensure proper identification and lifting of trace evidence. On a request by the NIA/StIA, the forensic laboratories will ensure that the tests are carried out and the report prepared overnight – unlike months for turnaround time as at present. The intelligence set-ups will also be ready to provide such information as is required or carry out 'searches' in their database or other tasks.

232 Sophisticated forensic laboratories in ample numbers, including brain-mapping centres, are required for the criminal justice system generally. Establishing these state-of-the-art laboratories with sufficient capacity will take time, but we can begin with a few, and they can give the first preference to terrorism-related forensic tests/reports.

233 To enable proper and effective investigation, the agency will need to be given wide powers and other statutory support. Here, even lie detector and brain mapping tests should not require legal consent. There are other parts of the investigation which fall in line with general criminal law and that is of forensics, telephone and cyber communication analysis and data, but all these only require more expertise and, of course, greater funds.

234 Finally, investigation of a terrorist act must be completed as soon as possible. The time factor is important for more reasons than one. First, with the lapse of every hour, the availability of more pieces of evidence, as also its authenticity, diminishes. Secondly, the arrestees may be in jail and it is not fair to take the cover of pending investigations to continue holding them in jail.

235 The IA and the support services should work as fast as is practically pos--sible, so that there is proper completion of investigation. Simply because the law provides for extension of the period for completing the investiga-

tion is no reason for not completing it at the earliest. The report should be submitted as early as possible, even if it does not cover the whole gamut of investigation. There can always be a supplementary report to the Court. To not proceed with utmost dispatch is just not acceptable.

236 For investigation, we need competent officers having a high level of both proficiency and integrity so that the possibility of an innocent being charged is minimal, and confined only to a case of bonafide error, and is not due to carelessness, overkill or corruption. While improving the police functioning on this score will generally take time, at least with the National Investigation Agency and its officers (as also the StIA), we can put in place an administrative set-up and culture that ensures minimal aberration on this account. It is necessary to do so because only then will the public and courts–and even the international community–carry full confidence in the investigations conducted by the NIA or StIA.

237 Like the intelligence outfits addressed in sub-topic 7, the agency would require more of trained investigators rather than be administrator heavy. To fight terrorism, we need the best possible quality of the former. Research and Training institutes for investigations and forensics is also necessary. Work is in progress to set up 20 investigator training schools.

Statutory and other support –6

238 Investigation of a terrorist attack (or even terrorism-related activity) is a daunting task where a number of officers and agencies need to be involved. Often, it needs to be divided into manageable sections–each working in coordination. It also (usually) requires extensive sifting, collating and analysis of data before coming to any meaningful conclusion. For this, the investigation agency needs statutory support to call for and receive information or documents, or even to get tasks done.

239 There are two parts here: the first is imposing a general duty on citizens to report suspicious activity at the pre-event level;[51] and the second (if an incident has occurred and investigations are in progress) is imposing a statutory duty on citizens to provide whatever information they have. Of the second, there are two sub-parts where the first sub-part (a new one) ought to be a general public notice (noting that the information is sought in relation to a terrorism-related investigation) calling for information from all persons who may be having it. If it is later found that someone had information which, despite such public notice, was not given, it would constitute an offence. The second sub-part is a specific summons to an individual, a corporate body or an organisation to furnish the required information.

240 An officer investigating a terrorist offence is empowered to issue summons to anyone in possession of relevant information to furnish such information or material to him. Once the summons specify that the information

51 provided there are systems to receive it, and it is done in a manner that does not cause harassment to the informant or expose him to some risks

being sought is in relation to a terrorism-related investigation, it should be sufficient to make the recipient work overtime, maybe all through the night, or for a bank or service utility company to specially open their office (even on holidays) so as to provide the required data / information, documents, etc. In short, compliance with such summons must have priority over all other work for the person/s concerned.

241 All institutions, business houses, corporations and other organisations should be required to render full support to the Investigation Officer, when called upon, even if it means deputing their record keepers and computer operators to assist the officers from the investigative team or help search for information which may be relevant. Photocopies or originals must be delivered. Further, the party be obligated to give the data as hard copy and as soft copy (to enable subsequent searching, correlation and processing by the investigating officer) and any claim for expenses incurred can follow later.

242 Failure to do so with full dispatch should entail a penalty. Moreover, the liability should attach not to the corporate (titular) head of the organisation, but to the corporation / organisation as an institution and also the person/s who were entrusted this specific task by the management. These provisions be equally applicable to the various Government departments and agencies. All Government offices must nominate an officer who would be responsible for making the files – or access to computer records – available to the NIA / StIA, even if it means working, like the private individuals or entities, overtime or on holidays.[52]

243 No doubt, failure to furnish information being made an offence is both harsh and capable of misuse. It may even alienate a part of the public from the investigating authorities. Therefore, harsh punishment should be limited to cases where the failure is intentional or designed to help the terrorists. Silence out of fear for one's life or other equally disastrous consequences should be construed as mitigating circumstances.

Statement before the court at the earliest – 7

244 This work expounds the concept of giving an opportunity to the accused to make a statement before the Magistrate at as early a point of time as possible – i.e., at the investigation stage. At this, the suspect / accused is expected to 'recollect' and describe the precise events and also account for his activities in a chronological order.[53] Answers to questions such as:

> Where were you, and what were your activities as also perceptions between two specified points of time? In whose company were you? Who is the owner of a particular article?

will be recorded. Explanatory or exculpatory facts may be included.

---

52 Such nominated officer will also be required to keep the contact numbers and other details of the officials / staff dealing with different subjects.

53 See the Form for a time sheet in sub-topic 6 of Topic 14, which can facilitate the accused in accounting for his activities between two points of time.

245 Sub-topic 6 of Topic 14 only proposes an 'opportunity', so that depending on the nature of the answers, the prosecution evidence could be appreciated and the strength of the presumption of innocence duly 'adjusted'.[54] However, to deal with terrorism, it requires going a step further. Here: (1) failure to explain should not only reduce the strength of the presumption of innocence, but do so to so little a point, that the belief evidence by a police officer could suffice to convict; and (2) the feasibility of making it compulsory for the accused to speak may be explored. See para 257 infra.

246 Recording witness's statements (examination-in-chief) in Court at the investigation stage itself (as argued for in sub-topic 7 of Topic 14) is also necessary. So done, the investigations and, thereafter, the trial can be much more focussed and effective.

247 Proceedings (during the course of investigations) of the type envisaged by Chapter XII of the Code will be taken up before the AT-Court and not before the Magistrate, except that recording the statement of the accused and the witnesses can be done before a Magistrate, provided he is so notified and empowered under the anti-terrorism law.

248 Grant of pardon to an approver may, in the exigencies of the situation, be a necessary evil. However, keeping in view the public sentiment, it will need to be cautiously handled. Similarly, Plea Bargaining (addressed in Topic 13) may also be permitted, but will require extra care.

Review Committee and charge sheet – 8

249 With investigation complete, the draft final report (charge sheet) be examined by a special Review Committee[55] in order to verify whether the case is one which should be proceeded under anti-terrorism laws before the AT-Courts, or under special or regular laws before regular courts. In other words, the first round of 'filtration' should be 'in-house' – the object being to avoid using the stringent law where it is not called for.

250 As noted in para 228 supra, the approach has to be one where on reasonable suspicion of there being a terrorist angle to any offence or event, the investigation is commenced by the StIA.[56] If it appears to be one having wide ramifications, the NIA may be requested to take over; and if the case turns out to be not one of terrorism, but something less, it will leave the local police to continue with their task. Even if the investigations are continued by the StIA, upon their conclusion, the Review Committee shall examine whether the accused are to be prosecuted under the AT-laws. If not, it will leave the matter to be prosecuted under other laws. See further discussion (and the schematic) in para 271 *et seq*.

54 The procedural tool of 'adjusting' the strength of the presumption of innocence is detailed in Topic 16.

55 This would be an improvised version of the Competent Authority to 'sanction' under the organised crime laws in force in some States.

56 A spot visit or some investigation by the SHO under the conventional procedures or even a preliminary enquiry may be required.

251 Only to illustrate, there could be ten cases investigated under AT-laws, but on completion of investigation, only three are found fit to be proceeded under AT-laws and the for the remaining seven, it is felt proper that they be prosecuted under the general laws. If the Review Committee decides to not proceed under the AT-law, it shall leave it to the regular police[57] to complete the remaining formalities, if any, and then file the report before the Magistrate of the area having jurisdiction, unless it be a case under some other special law that also requires filing before a Special Court.

252 Against the Review Committee's decision to proceed under AT-laws, no revision or any other petition would lie and the necessary safeguard is best provided by permitting a revision against the order of the Court framing the charge under AT-laws (see para 280 infra).

253 The report (charge sheet) submitted under AT-laws must be carefully structured – and segregated into parts for related offences – so as to facilitate the adducing of evidence at a multi-court trial as envisaged in para 331 *et seq*. It will be necessary where one offence is complete without the main event having taken place, except that the occurrence of the main event accentuates the culpability. Evidence on disputes of facts, which can be separately received (in an adjoining court), will be so received and all this can be done only if there has been proper structuring of the charge sheet.

254 Further, the charge sheet may withhold certain details – particularly those relating to the manner of getting to the evidence. Operational details ought not to be provided on the case file, as doing so would only compromise investigations. The names of the witnesses will need to be blanked out and they can be given code numbers instead of names. Procedures to submit the report in two parts, one open and the other in sealed cover, can also be explored. How much more detail is to be received in a sealed cover, or allowed to be made known to the accused, can be considered by the Court at the stage of framing the charge.

The 'fair' trial – 9

255 With the charge sheet filed, and before we proceed to address issues relating to the trial, we need to dwell upon certain fundamentals relating to criminal justice in this context. The first is the concept of a fair trial – addressed earlier in sub-topic 6 of Topic 7 at pp3~ supra. See in particular the discussion on which is the *fairest* trial from whose stand point at pp3~ supra.

256 Criminal laws and procedures must be such that the interest of the nation is not unjustifiably imperilled. Against this background, princeples of a fair trial also require that in appropriate cases, the interests of the defence of the nation are balanced against those of the society. The traditional rights and privileges of the accused need to be balanced against society's overall interest and safety from terrorism. The 'fair'

57 the SHO within whose jurisdiction the offence took place

needs to be considered in a more appropriate – or 'balanced' – perspective, where it is equally 'fair' to all concerned.

Right to silence –10

257 The privilege against self-incrimination haunts us for most crime, but how much it terrorises us in relation to this problem (terrorism) needs to be seriously looked at. Topic 8 of this chapter argues a case for abolition or, in any case, whittling down, of this privilege for general crimes. While that may require debate, when it comes to terrorism, there can hardly be any doubt. A positive obligation must be imposed by law on such accused persons to speak, and failure to account for their activities and perceptions may be defined as a separate offence. Such an approach would not transgress upon but only further the purposes of criminal justice. In any case, adverse inferences can also be drawn from failure to give evidence while still maintaining the presumption of innocence and the right to silence.

Reversing the Burden of Proof – 11

258 In many fields, over the past decade, criminal law has reversed the onus by requiring the accused – once certain facts are established – to prove his innocence. Taking a cue from there, AT-laws could require the accused to prove: (1) what his activities entailed; and (2) that they (his activities) were legitimate. Shifting the burden of proof onto the accused in certain circumstances is imperative.

259 To explain, the accused is presumed to be innocent. However, if there is a seizure of weapons or explosives, or incriminating documents are found, or communications are intercepted, the accused would have to prove his innocence. Several countries following the Common law system have also introduced provisions for placing the burden of proof on the accused (and also raising adverse inference), particularly after organised crime and terrorism shook nations worldwide.

Withholding Details –12

260 The fight against terrorism and terrorists will involve the increasing use of special techniques of intelligence and evidence collection. The question is: Should the techniques by which evidence is collected be disclosed at the trial? It is a fundamental principle of criminal jurisprudence that all 'papers' (copies) pertaining to oral and documentary evidence, as collected, are given over to the accused before the charges are framed. The fight against terrorism would however require some exceptions to be made in this regard. The main reason is that giving all papers could disclose the methods of evidence collection or the sources of information, which would then alert the other terrorists or terrorist organisations. Simply stated, a tool that could be used a dozen times thereafter is rendered useless.

261 Disclosure of evidence collection techniques will have to be protected or some of the evidence restricted only to the Judge, so that the means, methods or sources of surveillance and investigation do not become common knowledge and thus cease to serve their purpose in future. To take an illustration, if a prosecution witness, who is to prove an

intercepted communication between the accused and another, is allowed to be cross-examined by the defence counsel to the effect:

> What all methods did you employ for tapping the communication? When and how did you place the bug? By what method do you claim to have cracked the code and decrypted the communication? Which software did you use? Who all were involved in the team?

and the like, it would serve not criminal justice, but only the terrorists.

262 In the same way, informer privilege may involve more than merely refusing to divulge his name. Supporting evidence, which would be likely or might tend to disclose the identity of the informer, would itself be protected by such a privilege in the sense that it may not be allowed to be adduced under cross-examination. Recognition of legitimate public interest in protecting police sources of information, or the safety of informers or witnesses, has led to the acceptance of the possible justification of withholding relevant information from disclosure to the defence. There also exists a valid apprehension about the intimidation of witnesses, all of which can scuttle the trial process.

263 A judgment coming from a trained Judge, holding an accused guilty with-out referring to techniques of evidence collection in the judgment, will preserve of the value of the methodology for subsequent use. Despite the fact that the techniques of collection of evidence are not discussed, impartiality in evaluating evidence will have to be ensured. To do so, the Judge may 'cross-examine' the witness in camera and without making the answers a part of the record, record only his own view as to whether the evidence of the witness can be relied upon.

Confessions and Belief evidence –13

264 In criminal law, confessions before the police are not admissible in evidence. Confessions before senior police officers were admissible under TADA and POTA. However, despite the recent amendment, this is not so under UAPA. As a contrast, under laws relating to organised crime–which, as a shade of grey, fall short of terrorism – confession before a senior police officer is admissible in evidence. However, looking at the nature of the threat from terrorists, it is necessary that confession before police officers above a particular rank is made admissible in evidence. Similar is the case for admissibility of a confession by a co-accused. However, the Court would take extra care before giving credence to it.

265 Another procedural tool that can be explored is of making the 'belief evidence' of a police officer admissible. As practical experience shows, it is not always that all those involved are apprehended, or the requisite evidence reached and collected, wherefore trial procedures call for a different connotation. Even against those who are apprehended, absence of supporting evidence does not mean that they are factually innocent. The truth could be either misplaced suspicion or a case of factually guilty against whom there is no evidence.

266 Many people (witnesses) give information on condition of anonymity, which is not unjustified. There is also a situation where, like the pieces of a jigsaw puzzle, bits of information come from various sources and based on those, the investigation officer forms a belief, a strong one. Experience in this regard, therefore, renders it imperative that a statutory provision enable admissibility of 'belief evidence'. This, however, must come from the officer who was personally investigating and also vouched for by his supervising officer, so as to maintain credibility as far as possible. Moreover, reliance on such (belief) evidence may be restricted to cases where it is the officers of NIA or the StIA who give such evidence.[58]

267 The statement of belief, if made at the trial, can, given such a provision, be considered as evidence in the prosecution case against the accused. Like other evidence, it has to be weighed and considered, and the provision will not be construed as meaning that the trial court must convict the accused in the absence of exculpatory evidence.

268 Ultimately, and as a practice, the Court ought not to convict on the mere 'belief evidence', but there may be exceptional cases where the Court in its wisdom would be entitled to convict on this alone. These self-imposed restrictions by the Court will maintain the 'fair' trial. This exception, however, is made only because of the nature of the problem (terrorism) and may be extended to other serious problems like drugs, but cannot be extended to the traditional crime, be it a pick-pocketing on the street or a murder in the central market.

269 To the traditional jurists, an approach towards criminal justice as herein discussed might sound radical, but if we were to examine it further, it would not be a disproportionate response to the growing menace of global terrorism. After all, justice lies in rendering a judgment that approximates best with that which actually transpired. So much for the principles with regard to the approach.

Upon Cognizance, Retain or Transfer – 14

270 Coming back to the procedures, cases under anti-terrorism laws will not just be those relating to violent attacks; they will also relate to a number of other issues and offences, many of which will be not that serious, though they may well constitute a breach of law. Put differently, while the term 'terrorist' evokes a particular image, the various actors involved are not necessarily frontline operatives. Many would have committed offences which do not call for prosecution under AT-laws.

271 There has been misuse of anti-terrorism laws in the past, to prevent which, in addition to a Review Committee (as envisaged in para 249 supra), the AT-Court before which the charge sheet is filed will take cognizance and issue process. But the more important question is of 'considering' – and 'deciding' – whether to proceed under the (stringent) anti-terrorism

58 This is so by reason of administrative selection of, as also administrative discipline and control upon, such officers.

law (and before itself as an AT-Court) or send the matter to a regular court to be tried under: (1) the anti-terrorism laws; or (2) special laws of intermediate strength;[59] or (3) the regular laws. The schematic depicts the process:

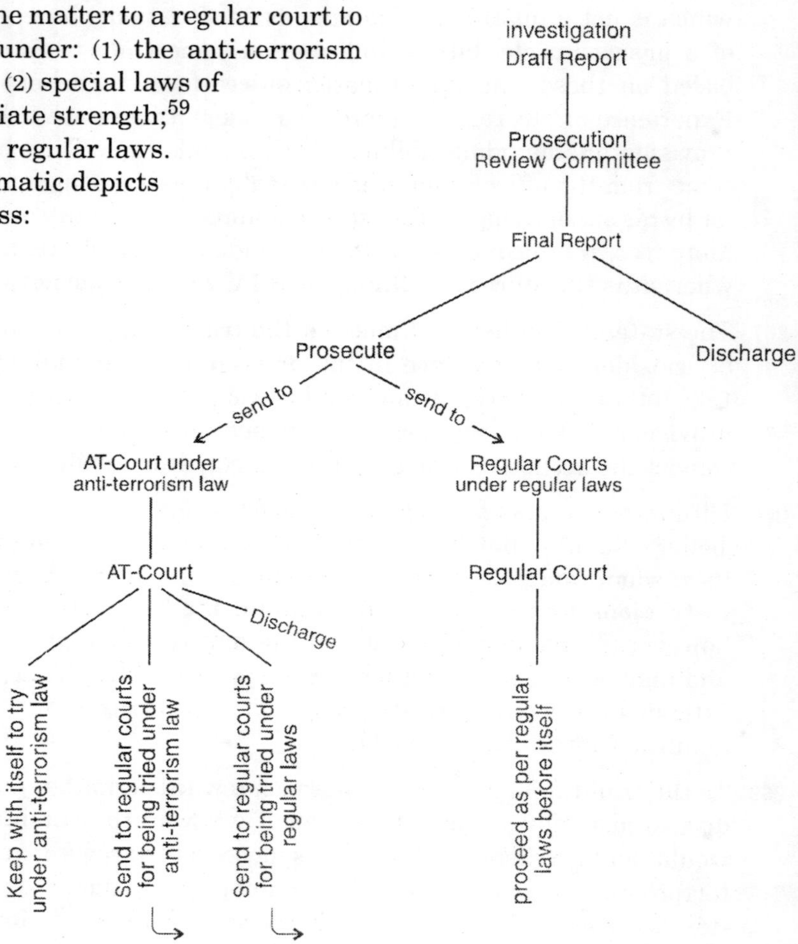

272 Elaborating on the above schematic in words, on conclusion of the investigations (and if the Review Committee so decides), the report (§ 173(2)) will be filed not before the Magistrate, but before the AT-Court.[60] The procedures of: cognizance (§ 190); issue of process (§ 204); supply of copy (§s 207/208); committal (§ 309), etc. shall then take place before the AT-Court, which shall be deemed to wield the powers otherwise exercisable by a Magistrate under the Code. After hearing the prosecution (and the defence) on the charge (§ 226); the AT-Court may either discharge the accused (§ 227); or keep the case with itself to try under AT-laws and proceed to frame charges (§ 228); or send the case to regular courts for being tried under: (1) AT-laws; or (2) special laws of intermediate strength; or (3) regular laws. For procedures to assail a decision to retain or transfer, see para 280 infra.

59 laws re: Organised crime, Public order, etc. In the schematic, the term 'regular laws' includes the laws having intermediate potency.

60 The symbol '§' denotes a 'Section' of the Cr.P.C. and has been used to save space.

273 In other words, like a Magistrate who, upon finding a case sessions triable, simply commits it to the Sessions Court under § 209 Cr.P.C. – or the Sessions Court sends it back to the Magistrate under § 228(1) – the AT-Court, upon finding that the prosecution need not be proceeded under the anti-terrorism law, or upon finding that it is not so serious so as to be tried before the AT-Court, may transfer the case to the regular court for bring tried under such laws as are appropriate for the case in hand. Similarly, if a regular Court (of Sessions or of the Magistrate) finds that the matter, though filed by the police directly before the Magistrate, is one that really needs to be tried by the AT-Court, or an offence under AT-laws appears to have been committed, it may refer the matter to the AT-Court for directions.[61] Occasions to do so will, however, be rare.

274 If the matter is retained by the AT-Court and proceeds to trial, the AT-Court, in addition to its powers under anti-terrorism laws, will also have the power of a Sessions Court under the Cr.P.C. If an offence under AT-laws is not proved, but if the prosecution does prove an offence under special or regular laws, a conviction may be returned. To remove doubts, it will need to be clarified that the AT-Court will have the power to convict those against whom the offence proved is not one under the AT-law but under special laws or regular laws. Similarly, the regular court (Court of Session only) would also be in a position (when so noted at the time of framing the charges) to return a conviction under AT-laws, for which purpose, it shall be deemed to possess and exercise the powers under AT-laws. A large number of offences, even if they be terrorist related, can, depending on the nature of the offence, be tried by a regular court.

275 The larger objective of this procedural pattern is twofold. Firstly, it will provide a second stage 'filter' and ensure that only those cases which disclose the need for prosecution and trial under stringent laws are so tried. It will give an opportunity to the accused to represent that he ought not to be prosecuted under the stringent laws, thereby preventing misuse by the police in wanting to treat a lesser offence as one under AT-laws.

276 Secondly, sending some AT-law trials to a regular court (Court of Sessions) becomes necessary as a practical measure. It will not unnecessarily burden the AT-Courts with cases which, though related to terrorism, are by and large such that they do not need the extra expertise (and expense) of the AT-Court and can well be tried by the regular courts. It will be something like shifting a not so critical patient from the ICU of a speciality hospital to the general ward of the civil hospital. Some terrorist trials require high security, extra infrastructure support and the bulk of the Court's attention only to that subject and case. Placing all trials before the AT-Court will cause overload, and that will defeat the purpose. In any case, the AT-Court and the regular court, or even the special court under

61 This is where the Court feels that the prosecution review committee was in error and it would be appropriate to charge the accused under AT-laws.

other stringent or medium stringency laws, are presided over by judicial officers of Sessions Judge rank.

Pre-trial procedures and framing charges –15

277 Continuing with procedures, many of the pre-trial procedures argued for in Topic 14 infra such as a specific 'response' to documents, which includes response to records of intercepted communication (whether oral, written or electronic), footage from surveillance cameras, comments on recovered items or case property, etc. (sub-topic 9); or response by the accused to the allegations of fact (sub-topic 10), will be necessary here. As propounded in sub-topic 11, the evidence of the formal witnesses can be received by way of an Affidavit-cum-Certificate. Whether it is records of money transfer, purchase of something, listing of phone calls, surveillance video footage, or a tape-recording or transcription of a voice recording, it can be received in advance and cross-examination permitted only where necessary. Forensic reports and expert evidence can be similarly received.

278 Pre-trial procedures now being complete, and while considering whether the case is to be proceeded under AT-laws and before the AT-Courts, or sent to regular courts, charges will have to be framed.

279 The charges can be framed in the pattern put forward in sub-topic 12 of Topic 14 infra as that would help bring out the facts that are admitted or established and those that require proof. It also helps to fix the onus (where it is upon the accused) with greater clarity. Further, if there be a large number of accused, and / or a large number of witnesses, the charges will also need to be framed in a manner that the adducing of evidence can be segregated, thus enabling multi-tasking – simultaneous recording of evidence before more than one court in a special court complex. Lastly, the provisions of Chapter XVII of the Code (particularly Sections 214 and 215) may require to be construed, more in keeping with the demands of the situation.

280 As noted in para 252 supra, the decision of the prosecution Review Committee to file the report under the AT-laws would not be challengeable, and it is only the decision of the Court (at the time of framing the charge) that would be a subject of revision. This will be similar to the revision as presently lies under Section 401 Cr.P.C. against framing the charge by any criminal court. A revision will then include the ground that such charge, if at all, should have been framed under regular laws and not under the AT-laws. Here, the State too would have a right to revision that a charge should have been framed under the AT-laws.

The Trial – 16

281 Charges having been framed, the trial begins. The pre-trial proceedings carried out, a detailed hearing and a clearer frame for the charges will give the trial a new dimension altogether, or simply make it much more focussed. Despite reversal of proof on certain issues, the prosecution must begin. The accused must be given his say, but it must be

remembered that the object of the trial is to reach the truth and with terrorism as the accusation, it has to be appropriately approached.

282 While the receiving of evidence by the courts is mandatory, the pattern and the manner of adducing evidence would need a re-look because against such an 'accused', not many witnesses would dare to openly come forward and depose. Also, the physical safety and, wherever necessary, anonymity, of witnesses has to be provided for.[62]

283 Appropriate systems and methods will have to be developed, of which one particular method deserves special mention, and that is of receiving the evidence of a witness without disclosing the witness's identity except to the judge. Legal provisions like cross-examination on video without the face being shown and with a voice-shift (electronic change) may have to be introduced.

284 In an extreme case, we may have to go still further. The witness's statement will need to be recorded at a separate (and secret) location. Power to do so must be provided, and after it has been recorded, the Judge can pass an order that it has been so done and record the reasons therefor. The right to cross-examine may, given sufficient reason, be declined, though the Judge, in order to reach the truth, must himself do the questioning in that direction. For arriving at a conclusion, only a limited weight is to be accorded to such evidence.

285 These are a few samples of how to achieve the purpose. Several other innovative and unusual methods for adducing and receiving evidence (some of which have been discussed in sub-topic 9 infra) will need to be recognised and enacted. Procedures will have to be tailored and novel methodology deployed for receiving evidence. Many more like these will evolve as experience is gained. After all, extraordinary situations require extraordinary and innovative solutions. Sub-topic 9 (para 320 *et seq*) further addresses trial procedures and functioning of the AT-Courts.

286 One word more. It is not always that all accused are before the Court as some may be absconding. The procedural law will need to take care of this aspect as well so that a judgment against such accused is neither made difficult nor capable of being found technically flawed.

The judgment, and graded finding of guilt – 17

287 Recording of evidence concluded; arguments addressed; the judgment is reserved and awaited. The judgment will need to meet all norms of criminal jurisprudence. Apart from those relating to admissibility, there are also principles for appreciating the evidence and then coming to a conclusion of guilt or otherwise. The principles in this regard – beyond reasonable doubt vis-à-vis preponderance of probabilities; let 100 guilty go free but not let one innocent be punished; and the like – have been addressed in Topic 15 of this chapter. Topic 16 propounds a new tool – of

62 See the discussion on Witness Protection Programme in Topic 19 sub-topic ~.

adjusting the strength of the presumption of innocence depending on the tenor of the response at the earliest opportunity given to account for and explain his whereabouts, activities, perceptions, possessions, etc.

288 Procedural tools and approaches as these will bring some respite to criminal justice, but would not be enough. While the requirement of evidence can be reduced, the onus reversed, appropriate inferences from silence drawn, and other measures taken to achieve the results, keeping in view the nature of the activity (terrorism), there will still be many cases of a correct accusation but too little proof to warrant a conviction, particularly when the punishment that follows is severe. Many factually guilty, or involved with terrorism in some way or the other, will continue to escape punishment. This 'grey area' is vast and needs to be catered to.

289 The prosecutions under the AT-laws will not be only against those carrying out violent attacks in which they failed and were captured, but by the very nature of things, will be also against many others. Apart from the actual perpetrator, the conspirators, financiers, harbourers and those who provided logistic support, there could be those who played only peripheral roles in the process. There will also be those who got involved unknowingly, were unknowingly 'used', or committed a technical breach of law. Of this large number as accused, many will have only little evidence against them and will fall in a grey area, and with varying shades in between.

290 In the past, TADA & POTA were criticised for the large number of unwarranted arrests. Of those arrested, only a few were formally charged and tried, and of those few, most were acquitted. Proceeding on principle, rather than on empirical data, such criticism seems to be partly correct, partly unjustified and also somewhat of an exaggeration. True, an unduly large number of arrests were made, but the 'extra number' was partly because of misuse and partly by reason of absence of laws of intermediate strength. In fact, in many cases, the arrest and the subsequent release (without trial) was of a person who was a criminal, though not a terrorist, and had therefore served its purpose, i.e., reigning in the deviant.

291 Also, of those charged and tried under TADA and POTA, many of the acquittals were of the factually guilty. As a rough indicator, and only to put forward the point: Out of the notional 100 against whom charges were framed,[63] 90 were acquitted, and of which 90, 2 were falsely charged, 58 were criminals but not terrorists, and 30 were terrorism-related offenders (or involved in terrorism) against whom sufficient evidence could not reach the record. Apart from these, there were also many who deserved to be proceeded against under these laws, but were either not (or could not be) arrested; or even if arrested, were released for want of sufficient evidence.

63 We are ignoring those who were initially arrested under these laws, but later released without having to face a trial.

292 It must be remembered that evidence against a terrorist, accomplices of terrorists, or those persons who indulge in acts supportive of terrorism or who are simply involved, but only to a very small extent, is difficult to come by. Similarly, where conspiracy and abetment is to be proved, direct evidence is seldom available, and it is necessarily a matter of inference. Regarding admissibility of evidence, loosened standards prevail in a conspiracy trial.[64] Many times, it may not even qualify to be 'proof' as known to traditional criminal jurisprudence.

293 Often, with such as the case file, the Judge is convinced in his mind that the accused was involved and is guilty, yet in the absence of legal evidence, he has no option but to acquit the accused. With the statute providing for severe punishment, often with a 'minimum', it becomes difficult for the Judge to hand down a conviction.

294 As procedural reform, to cover the inevitable difficulties in our criminal investigations and criminal justice system (as also some of the failings), this work, in Topic 17 of this chapter, argues a case for putting in place procedures for graded finding of guilt (or classes of guilt) – as Class A, Class B or Class C. If there be some evidence against an accused, but not enough, instead of an acquittal (as at present), a conviction in Class B or Class C may be returned and followed by a punishment which does not extend to include incarceration, and is directed more towards civil penalties, compensation, and S-restraints and C-surveillance, i.e., prevention.

295 While this procedural tool (of graded finding of guilt) is required to be used across all types of offences, it will be particularly useful in terrorism-related prosecutions. Those accused against whom the evidence falls short of the mark can then, instead of being acquitted, be convicted in an alternative (lower) class whereafter limited, especially 'preventive', punishment (see paras 313 to 316) can be meted out. Particularly seeing the harsh punishment that would follow, to convict one who could possibly be innocent and, at the same time, to acquit one who is, in all probability, guilty, but not so beyond reasonable doubt, presents a serious problem. The ability to return a finding of guilt in Class B or Class C will provide both a useful tool and also help strike a better balance between competing forces.

296 The judgment ought to be carefully structured, for often, many are involved, with the role of each varying in degree and intent. See the discussion on structuring the criminal courts' judgment in Topic 15 infra. Further, if the size of the record be huge, the page numbering system put forward in Topic 6 of Chapter 14 infra, with cross-reference to the page number within square brackets, is essential. It helps the appellate court, in fact any reader, even the convicted.

---

64 *Firozuddin Basheeruddin vs State of Kerala*
2001-7 SCC 596 = AIR 2001 SC 3488

297 Against the judgment, one appeal must be permitted. At a trial under AT-law, if there be several accused where any one is convicted under the AT-law, and the other accused are convicted not under AT-laws but under regular law, an appeal ought to lie only to the court to which an appeal against the decision of the AT-Court lies. Similarly, in the event of lesser conviction or an acquittal, the State (prosecuting agency) will be able to appeal against the judgment to the court where appeals against the AT-Court would lie. Finally, the appeal must be heard and disposed of without delays. See Section 21 of the National Investigation Agency Act.

A different procedure for Sentencing – 18

298 With terrorism-related matters, sentencing, which follows soon after conviction, will also require a new approach, and one contrary to the current criminal jurisprudence where the Court becomes *functus officio* after sentencing. For dealing with terrorists whose acts do not warrant the imposition of a death sentence, an offbeat approach is required. Offbeat in the sense that there will have to be a continual varying of the severity of the punishment after the conviction – a concept presently unknown to our criminal jurisprudence.

299 A person convicted under AT-laws is not only the one who came on a suicide mission and was arrested. There will be very many convicted for lesser wrongs. There would be those who are otherwise good people, but who made a mistake or got swayed. In a democratic society, to send each of them to jail for a minimum of, say, seven, years is not correct. The punishment prescribed is severe, and often with a minimum. In many ways, the 'minimal' actually defeats the purpose because on the one hand, it makes it difficult to hand down a conviction,[65] and on the other, if the accused is convicted, oftentimes, it overly punishes.

300 The punishment would have to vary, depending on the nature of the act and the precise role. The offences can take various forms and shapes and there can be degrees of gravity, so the statute has to cover the whole gamut, but the prosecution as also the courts will have to impose punishment only as much as is necessary and no more. There are two parts here. One is the kind and extent of punishment and the other (if it be a long term in prison) is to consider suspension while the convict can be released on probation, subject to S-restraints and C-surveillance.

301 Upon release, depending on the conduct of the convict, and if promise is shown, the probation can be continued from time to time. If there is a change in the situation for the better, and after some years, there can even be 'remission', which is commuting the sentence. The overall objective is to maintain effective deterrence, and more so because many of the convicts would be indoctrinated and misled minds.

302 If there is re-emergence of activities or revival of support for terrorism, the suspension is revoked and the convict is called upon to serve the

65 See the discussion in para ~ of Topic 17 at pp3~ infra.

original sentence in full. In such an event, the law may provide that the period of probation will not be counted towards the total sentence if the convict shows bad conduct at any time thereafter.

303 Finally, in sentencing, a difference between the 'hardcore' and the 'swayed' terrorist has also to be maintained. The latter has to be exposed to an overdose of education, vocational training, and work or gainful occupation while in prison, and, as time goes by, increasing spells of parole with constant reporting. The unemployed and misguided youth who are the main source of recruitment for terrorist organisations have to be ultimately brought back into the mainstream.

304 Looked at in another way, while one part is reducing the possibility of convicting an innocent person, unlike with other crime, with terrorism, there are many persons who may fall in the net – and for things as simple as unknowingly assisting. Often, these are otherwise law-abiding citizens who genuinely feel that they were in the right and the government was in the wrong. In all such cases, imposing a sentence, but deferring its serving out or allowing controlled probation, will work far better than the present system of minimum sentence for a term in prison, where too, the percentage of conviction is dismal.

305 Topic 18 (Penology) includes discussion on the Probation of Offenders Act. Although an overlap with surveillance, accounting and reporting as discussed here, a carefully structured, separate 'Probation of Offenders (Terrorism-related Offences) Act' is necessary for those who get involved with terrorism more as a mistake or to make a little profit from some transaction (which came to be associated with terrorism) and thereafter realised their mistake. If they are first-time offenders, often below the prescribed age, and carry hope to be law-abiding citizens in the future, then a 'release' on probation would perhaps be beneficial.

306 Unfortunate as it is (and like with narcotics / drug-related crimes), juveniles who get involved with terrorism – even if as 'victims' in the humane sense – do not always deserve the leniency under the Juvenile Justice (Care and Protection of Children) Act [56 of 2000]. A statutory exception has to be inserted therein.

Death Sentence –19

307 The death penalty (capital punishment) is a subject matter of debate worldwide. However, when dealing with terrorism, the death sentence need not be confined to the rarest of rare case. Where there is evidence beyond reasonable doubt, death penalty should be readily imposed. One reason is that restricting or converting it to a life sentence often results in a (unintended) 'death sentence' to innocent in the society, i.e., those who could then be taken hostage – and even killed – in order to secure the terrorists' release from prison.[66] See the discussion in Topic 18 infra.

66 Delaying the trial has a similar effect.

308 One word more. When it comes to punishment for those against whom involvement in terrorist activities is proved beyond doubt, even a death penalty may be inadequate.[67] Other forms of 'harsher' punishment that would appear to work against terrorism may have to be thought of and adopted. The traditional mindset of fairness should not come in the way. In this context, it may be noted that Article 7 of the International Covenant on Civil and Political Rights, 1966 was conceived at a time when terrorism was not even born. In the ensuing four decades, the terrorists, by their own acts and deeds, have carved out an exception. It is time civilised society recognises and applies that exception.

Continued 'Preventive' Detention –20

309 In para 171 supra, the need for preventive detention was addressed. Despite sounding contradictory in terms, in the fight against terrorism, we also need to put in place a variant – 'Preventive Detention as a sequel to trial'. Basing itself on the procedural tool propounded in Topic 17 infra, paras 294 & 295 supra argue that in a typical criminal prosecution where the evidence falls short of the mark, the accused may be convicted not in Class A, but in Class B or Class C, and meted out punishment in the form of a civil penalty or milder restraints. However, if the offence be terrorism-related and there be some evidence (if not enough), in the event of a Class B conviction, the AT-laws ought to permit continued imprisonment under the label of 'preventive'.

310 A term for preventive detention is usually for one year, extendable at best by one more year and no more, and is, even otherwise, not 'rigorous' imprisonment. Parole can be more readily given. Stated simply, if the persuasive force of the prosecution evidence is not sufficient to warrant a conviction in Class A (with severe punishment), but there is enough ma--terial to warrant a conviction in Class B, the AT-Court, in an appropriate case, may (while convicting in Class B) direct preventive detention.

***Prisons* – 21**

311 Prisons are another problem area. The present practice of using the general prisons or the high security cell in a general prison for housing both terrorists and other criminals is wrong. Separate prisons for housing those arrested or convicted under the anti-terrorism laws are required, with built-in segregation for the undertrials and convicts.

312 The system of detention in the same prison, particularly of youth who have strayed, is also wrong. A separate prison is required to house them. Involving them in vocational training and work rehabilitation coupled with professional counselling while restraining their contact with the outside world is also essential as it can prove to be an effective antidote to their alienated mindset.

***Ordering S-Restraints and C-Surveillance* – 22**

313 As noted in para 173 supra, two tools, more preventive in nature, but deployed as a 'punishment', are Special Restraints and Continued

67 Most of them are themselves ready for a suicide attack.

Surveillance. Stemming from the procedural tool of graded finding of guilt (paras 294 & 295 supra), where there is some evidence, but not enough, S-restraints and C-surveillance will help justice in this field to strike the right balance – be effective and yet not so unfair to the innocent or the swayed who get entangled.

314 The first – S-restraints – is a form of control order (described in Topic 18 at pp3~ infra), enabling imposition of conditions on the one convicted but not sent to prison. This can include prohibiting him from using specific items or services (such as the Internet); monitoring his association with specific people; imposing limitations on movement, curfews or house arrest; compelling him to wear an electronic tag at all times; fitting his home with such equipment as may be considered necessary to ensure compliance; and the like. A direction for compulsory relocation of a person and for his movement to be restricted to a particular area can also be a method that can be tried.

315 Other methods can be conceived and put in place. Conditions imposed under a control order will be tailored to each case to ensure that the person cannot take part in any terrorist activity. Doing so will enable far better control by the Authorities and also impose restraints (short of incarceration) that serve the purpose, while maintaining a balance.

316 In somewhat similar strain, continued comprehensive surveillance, including reporting, is generally understood to be a tool in the hands of the executive in the preventive realm. Topic 18 infra argues for its additional use as a post-conviction order in which case it comes to bear the punitive trappings. In tackling terrorism, this tool, both in its preventive form at the instance of the executive and in its punitive form (consequent upon trial before a Court and a conviction even if it be in Class C) can be very effective and useful, particularly against those who would otherwise be acquitted and thus emboldened to continue. In the fight against terrorism, preventive surveillance as also post-incident investigation calls for a new dimension.

Coordinating with other laws – 23

317 The anti-terrorism statute, howsoever wide it may be, cannot on its own effectively deal with terrorism. It will need much more. First, general improvement in the criminal justice system is required. Next is enacting separate laws relating to Organised Crime and Public Order, so that for cases which fall within their ambit, anti-terrorism laws are not used. Required alongside are laws on Corruption (Topic 4) and Proceeds of Crime and Money Laundering (Topic 5). It will need attention of very many other laws, statutes and rules, even ostensibly unrelated ones.

318 Thereafter 'links' with related laws have to be given so that the anti-terrorism laws are neither viewed in isolation nor does the presence of too much legislation on the subject stifle their effect. This would enable

effective handling of those (minor) offences that have a bearing on terrorism, but cannot by themselves be regarded as terrorist acts.

319 Insofar as procedures are concerned, some of the procedural reform argued for in the various sub-topics of Topic 14 could be taken as a base and then duly tailored to give the trial and adjudication under AT-laws the necessary efficacy. So can some of the thoughts placed in Topics 12, 13, 15, 16 and 17. In the end, it needs not just a stiff substantive law, but also efficient procedures for trial. The field being wide, this is only a part and there will be many more issues to be attended to, so that a fine set of substantive and procedural laws is put in place.

9. Courts–super fast-track

320 Prosecution and trial of cases takes time. This involves different kinds of times – 'Processing Time'; 'Waiting Time'; 'Hearing Time'; and 'Adjudicating Time'.[68] There is also, in our court proceedings, a substantial amount of 'Wasted Time', which is only another way of describing the inefficiencies. With terrorism-related prosecutions and trials (and special courts therefor), the aforesaid 'times' need to be appropriately looked at.

321 Speedy trials under anti-terrorism laws are important for the reasons that: (1) there is limited availability of evidence; (2) there exists a risk of attack on soft targets to secure the release of those accused as terrorists; and (3) the very nature of the law and its purpose calls for it. Certainty and speed are essential for ensuring the efficacy of the trial process as also of the punishment.

322 It is necessary that the trial under anti-terrorism laws be carried out and completed on a super fast-track basis[69] – which calls for establishing more courts and providing additional infrastructure and support staff, including prosecutors. While the processing time – as compared to general litigation – should be reduced, the 'waiting time' here should be next to nil, that is to say if a trial can (theoretically) conclude within one month, it should conclude within that one month; no adjournments for whatever reason should be granted. The Court should have only that matter on board and may even, by way of an example, work overtime to conclude the statement of a witness. For speedy trials, the hearing should preferably be on a day-to-day basis. Further, the hearings may be in camera, i.e., closed to the public.

---

68 The Waiting time (i.e. waiting for the given date to arrive as also waiting on that day for the court to spare time and for the hearing to begin) has been addressed in Chapter 1 (Topic 3 at pp5 and Topic 5 at pp 71, 79 and 80); Chapter 6 (Topic 1 at pp392); and Chapter 7-07 (Topic 9 at pp1499). Chapter 7-10 (Adjournments) also contains several references thereto. These 'times' are further addressed in Topic 1 (sub-topic 5) of Chapter 12 – Case and litigation Management.

69 See the discussion on fast-track courts in Topic 3 (sub-topic 2) of Chapter 12 infra.

323 Against the final judgment, appeals (whether by the State or by the accused) ought to be heard with topmost priority. Unless such (super fast-track) courts are established, the fight against terrorism will be incomplete.[70] A few thoughts on the composition, pattern, procedures and practices of these courts follow.

324 The AT-Courts will need, in addition to the power for trial of any offence under the special statute/s, to have all powers of the Court of Sessions as also a Magistrate under the Cr.P.C. and also the power to try for breach of other laws, provided they have nexus to terror. The greater objective is that all concerned tasks can be carried out before the same court.

325 These (AT-) Courts will be special in many ways, such as selected judicial officers, may be more than one judicial officer, support staff, a conglomeration of courts, specific location, etc. The judicial officers who are to preside over the AT-Courts (as super fast-track or special courts) can be selected by the High Court from the Sessions Judges in that State or even another State,[71] keeping in view the difficult situations that are faced in these trials. While remaining totally fair to all concerned, the AT-Courts will have to carry an aura of strictness and 'no nonsense' in expeditiously conducting the trials.

326 We might even need to set up a central cadre of Judges (of District Judge rank) who will receive regular training and continuing education, for the trial of such offences, at a Central Academy. While continuing to do their other judicial tasks, (when required for terrorism-related cases) they can, upon being directed by the High Court, preside over the AT-Courts.

327 For prosecutors too, there will need to be, once again, a central cadre of those who have received (and continue to receive) special training on the subject. The prosecutor's office also needs to have adequate support staff and equipment, integral to its establishment.

328 Full use of technology has to be made. The entire record, including the exhibits, may be made available as a computer (searchable) file, which shall also carry the page numbers of the printed record. The photographs may appear as digital images (JPEG) on the screen and have captions which can be searched through. For video or voice transcripts, adding sub-titles at the bottom (in advance) will make both searching and assimilation by the Judge much easier. Even animated motion pictures/videos of how the terrorist act was carried out can be prepared.[72]

---

70 Many of the points noted in this sub-topic have been addressed by the National Investigation Agency Act [34 of 2008] and the amendments to the Unlawful Activities (Prevention) Act [37 of 1967].

71 If they are from another State, it would require intervention of the Central Government or clearance by the Supreme Court.

72 This will not be very different from what TV channels now show except that the one before the Court has to be absolutely accurate and unbiased.

329 For instance, in surveillance footage that records both audio and video, we can always have an additional copy in which on the upper three-fourths of the screen, the video appears, and on the lower one-fourth screen, there is a transcript of the spoken words (in original language as also the translation in English). On these lines, a number of technological and presentation aids can help facilitate, as also speed up, the trial process.

330 Another peculiar feature of such trials is the large number of accused involved, for a terrorist activity is not restricted to just the man in the front; there is a whole chain or team behind him. They would have had all kinds of roles – some knowingly, some half-knowingly and others unwittingly. There are those who may have provided funds or logistic support, or those who transported material / people. There could be the banker through whom the funds were transferred and who failed to report; or the taxi driver who, upon seeing a customer no different than any other and lured by a 500 Rupee tip in advance, went out of his way without realising what the passenger was up to; and the like. With proper investigations carried out, to find a hundred persons arraigned may not be impossible.

331 Trials as these last not just for a year, but for more than a decade. Presently, apart from other inefficiencies, with a large number of accused, witnesses and lawyers, the productivity of a typical court, at the end of the day, is low. To tide over this situation, there is an innovation which could be tried. Although the practice of recording evidence in three different matters before the same court at the same time is common, we need to toy with the concept of formally splitting a trial and then holding (for the splinter/s) separate trials simultaneously in separate but adjoining courtrooms presided over by different Judges. At the end, a combined final judgment covering all aspects can be rendered.

332 To expatiate, if the number of accused and witnesses be large, at times, it will be worthwhile to split the trial (into many small ones), particularly when the role of a particular accused is substantially separate or only a finding on proof of fact/s has to be returned, which can be done separately. After an Order splitting the trial into parts, say, five, is passed, a conglomeration of (separate) courts will carry out the task of receiving, segregating and collating the evidence; hearing arguments and contentions of the two sides; returning a finding of fact or only recommending a finding of fact; and then placing the record (together with an interim judgment or recommendation) for consideration before the main Court for formal and final disposal.

333 A 'part' trial as this could include the trial against some accused who may not have been fully involved, but were associated in some minor way. These could include transporters; money launderers; or persons who provided shelter, food, phones, logistic support, etc; or others. Such role by itself would constitute an offence, whether or not the main accused are convicted. As another example, during the investigation of a terrorist

act, if prohibited arms & ammunitions or explosive materials are found, the possessor can be prosecuted separately, specially where the offence was complete, irrespective of whether the main event (terrorist attack) had taken place or not.

334 The additional/associate courts can receive evidence on a particular issue alone, and return a finding of fact (as distinct from conviction), which can then be sent to the main court for further consideration. Receiving the evidence and adjudication of peripheral issues in a manner as aforesaid (or by many courts put together) will enable an early end to the trial. Otherwise, it takes years and the whole purpose is lost.

335 Our criminal trials are not before a Jury which has to assemble and 'hear' every bit of witness statements (evidence) before returning a verdict. It is a ground reality that in our courts, when the evidence is being received, the attention of the Judge is more towards seeing that it is accurately recorded[73] and not on assimilating it for the purposes of final adjudication. It is only at the time of final arguments that the evidence recorded is 'read through', at which point of time the Judge grasps it (evidence) for the purposes of understanding and adjudication.

336 The role of the Court in observing the demeanour of the witness during the course of trial so as to form an opinion as to his truthfulness or otherwise has, over the last century, diminished to near zero. If we were to conduct a small experiment by asking the typical criminal court (which recorded the entire evidence) to hear final arguments and decide without reading through the evidence at that time,[74] most courts will simply be unable to do so. In other words, it is at the reading of the evidence at the time of final arguments that a typical Judge pays attention, understands, assimilates, and on the basis of that, proceeds to decide.

337 A trial in this form may be objected to on the ground, amongst others, that the accused and the defence counsel can only be present at one place at a time, but the problem being what it is, practical considerations require that all such objections be overruled and the accused be left free to appoint another counsel or get one from the Legal Aid Cell. The problem by its very nature is terrorising enough to carve for itself an exception to the rationale behind 317 Cr.P.C.–so long as the evidence of two witnesses on the same point is not being recorded.

338 The final judgment will, of course, be written by the Judge-in-charge, but it will be countersigned by the companion Judges and Magistrates who can also be, in a way, 'assisting parties' to it, the role of each being limited. This pattern may be wholly different from the traditional form where a single Judge signs, or in a Bench of two or more, all Judges are of an

73 and, at times, ruling upon its admissibility/relevance and also ensuring that the witness is not browbeaten

74 or by mentally ignoring the evidence that was recorded

equal level. There can be a legend at the end as to which section (paras) of the judgment was written by which Judge / Magistrate. Of course, the responsibility will rest with the Judge-in-charge who must concur or render his own judgment on these 'semi-separately tried' charges.

339 To enable trials in this form, the High Court may select several Judges, as also Magistrates, to conduct such a trial and appoint a senior Judge as the Judge-in-charge, to whom all facilities of a Case Manager and other infrastructural support will be provided. Now, these two or more Judges (along with Magistrates) will hold court in relation to the same terrorist offence, so that there are, say, four or five courts being held simultaneously in a court complex. The responsibility is with the Judge-in-charge who records evidence on crucial matters while peripheral issues, receiving other evidence and carrying out other formalities is done before the other courts presided over by the associate Judges / Magistrates. The Judge-in-charge will also need to be given greater freedom to lay down or adopt procedures and practices that differ from the conventional.

340 As part of trial management, if there be a large number of accused, a system of signing (thumb-marking) on a pre-printed form could save the time consumed in recording the presence of the accused and the counsel. Other forms of innovations, procedures and practices so as to utilise the court time and reduce impediments will also have to be put in place. Further, with voluminous record, competent and confidential secretarial assistance, which ensures proper file management, double-checking and cross-referencing, is also called for. It is a system and procedures as these which are required. See further discussion on carrying out Complex trials in sub-topic 13 of Topic 13 infra.

341 Whatever more we may have to do, it is to be ensured that the trial is completed and the final judgment rendered well within one year. A trial which does not culminate within one year will fail to serve the purpose of justice. With every unit of delay beyond six months, firstly, the trial loses out on effectiveness and sends out a wrong message to the terrorists; and secondly, delays entail direct and indirect costs, which are far more than what it would take to speed up and conclude the trial within a few months.

342 In this manner, and along with appropriate systems to provide for the operation and functioning of this conglomeration of courts, the trial of a terrorist offence (incident), which would have lasted a decade (as a few cases in the past have shown), can be concluded well within a few months and with far greater accuracy in the end result. The concept being novel, it will have to be first developed and then deployed. Inasmuch as the need for this kind of 'multi-tasking' arises only on a few occasions a year in the country – if it is a terrorist act or a large scam – an approach as this is but imperative.

343 There is also the question of location of these courts. While murder prosecutions and trials can be carried on in any of the 500-odd district courts in the country, for terrorism-related prosecutions, we need special courts – not only by the name (and experience and skills of the Presiding Officers), but also in terms of the security and other infrastructure, and the location. Perforce, such courts (complexes) in the country can be only a few wherefore power with the Government (with the concurrence of the High Court) to notify a court at a particular location, even if it in be a different State, is also called for. Proximity to the High Court, and good rail and air connectivity is essential. We can build a few court complexes of this type at various locations in the country with accompanying infrastructure, and then shift terrorism-related trials to such courts.

344 In short, establishing sufficient number of courts presided over by trained Judges and duly supported by infrastructure is essential. Alongside (and as noted above) is the need for such courts to follow procedures and practices as are tailored to the subject – terrorism.

10. The role of the Media

345 Terrorism, rather the reporting of it, has found the media, both print and electronic, involved. For the orchestrators, it is this 'news' of the event which is of greater importance than the injury to unknown innocents as the wide publicity it gives to their (terrorists') acts, and the resultant fear psychosis and breakdown of public security, is exactly what they want. Further, the media's manner of sensationalising the 'news', in an unintended effect, provides support to the terrorists who do not deem their act/s to be complete unless it is fully blown up by such publicity.

346 For the media to portray a terrorist (or a terrorist chief) – often with his picture – is not 'denouncing' him, but only adding to his prowess. There are a few terrorists whose faces are more familiar (courtesy the media) to a typical young one than the faces he should actually be familiar with. This publicity not only fulfils the aim of terrorism but also provides sufficient motivation to others to join the bandwagon of terrorism.

347 There are 100,000 road accident deaths in the country annually. How much print space and TV time is devoted to these? Similarly, there are 50,000 murders in a year. How much media coverage does each murder get? But when it comes to a terrorist attack, the amount of print space and TV time they get – as also the manner of reporting – needs no elaboration. It is this which creates a fear psychosis and erodes the authority of the State – and this is the very goal of those behind the attack, rather than any enmity with those killed or injured. Consequent to a terror attack, a report confined to a terse: "This this happened. It is being dealt with," will sound strange, but it will serve a greater purpose.

348 The media needs to impose upon itself restrictions of not publishing the name, photograph or identity of a terrorist, and if it has to report anything,

then a bland mention of the incident and 'one terrorist' should suffice. A display of a caricature representing him as more of a monster and not a photograph of the actual terrorist – or his suspected leader – will go a long way. Once a terrorist knows that even if he succeeds in his mission, there will be no publicity, he may be deterred from crossing this Rubicon.

349 Then, an attempt by a section of the media – particularly some TV channels – to find fault with the investigation creates a halo of martyrdom around those suspected of having committed these crimes. If such a person is either arrested or killed in an encounter, grieving relatives are shown vou--ching for his innocence and putting forward opinions against the police, which are freely projected, while the police is compelled to maintain silence regarding the available evidence in the interest of the investigation.

350 The minute-to-minute reporting of the rescue missions, and of the various movements and activities of the intelligence and investigation outfits – who went where, who met whom, who did what, and the like – does incalculable damage. So does reporting the methodologies and technology deployed for intelligence-gathering, surveillance, investigation or otherwise tackling the problem of terrorism. Unnecessary cross-examination by the media makes the task difficult. There is no reason why reporting cannot wait till the trial is complete.

351 There is, at other times, attempt to discredit the army, security forces, and local investigations in an endeavour to project the terrorists as victims of police misadventures. In the race for 'we were able to report, and report first', the real loser is the potency of Government forces and investigation teams. In short, the media, which imparts news, in practical effect (and unintendedly), ends up giving terrorism much of the oxygen it needs.

352 Take another instance as it happened with the recent Mumbai episode. It was widely reported that the intelligence inputs received were not acted upon. Such reporting, and the blame game of why the agency did not act, in the electronic media and the newspapers will only ensure that the next time, the wrongdoers will be more careful;[75] there will be no intelligence input; and there will be no occasion for the agencies to act upon it.

353 Apart from minimising the coverage and holding back reports on the progress of investigations, at times, it may be necessary for the media to even aid the authorities by 'planting' information so as to help apprehend the other terrorists involved. Let us take an illustration of this. Assume a terrorist attack (say, the one at Mumbai on 26.11.2008) was in progress. If the media, instead of reporting the way it did, had refrained, it is one thing. But if it had (in concert with the command forces), gone further and broadcast (false) 'news' to the effect:

---

75 for now they know where they had failed (in not being able to keep some of their communications / activities as secret as they thought they had), but were plainly lucky that no follow-up action was taken on the intelligence agencies' input

> Four terrorists have been arrested and have been housed at such & such police station and are being interrogated, OR are being sent to such & such place via this this this route for a lie detector test.

their comrades' probable attempt to free them, or the movements of the conspirators monitored electronically or otherwise (TECHINT or HUMINT), could have gone a long way in helping nab the others involved.

354 To do so would be no different than the dropping of metal foil by one Allied plane (in order to give an impression of hundreds of warplanes approaching from that direction) during the Second World War, which, when picked up by the radars, sent the Nazi forces to that (wrong) direction while the attack came from another side. But, it is not the media alone. Others have also to understand. In the present-day situation, if such a thing had been done, let alone crediting the NSG and its command officers for their strategy in nabbing the other conspirators, it (officers) would only be accused by the Human Rights activists of causing custodial deaths. There are times and situations where we need to be more practical than theoretical and this is just one example.

355 The 'right to know' and the media's duty is important and must be respected, but when such 'information' ends up fuelling the terrorists' game plan, an exception must be carved out. In the long-term interest of public safety and security, it may, at times, be necessary to constrict the 'right to know'. A related problem is that after an unfortunate incident, leaders make statements with the object of gaining political mileage, which are widely picked up and reported. They too need to refrain from making such statements, for all this only does harm to the nation. In other words, like many things in our country, handling the terrorists who have been nabbed has been unnecessarily politicised, and so despite the fact that it compromises our national security.

356 Self-restraint on this score by the media will deprive the terrorist of the prize they seek – i.e., glory. Difficult as it may sound, if self-restraint does not work, media reporting of such acts may require to be curbed or controls put in place as a part of the fight against terrorism. It is only a matter of balancing competing claims – all in the interest of citizen safety.

11. Funding the effort

357 Lastly, we come to the question of funding the effort against terrorism. The question of allocating funds for law-making has been addressed in Topic 2 of Chapter 9 at pp2~ supra; for courts generally in Topic 2 of Chapter 14 infra; and for the police and the criminal justice system in sub-topic 2 of Topic 19 infra. On this score (terrorism), let us first assess the value of the injury that we suffer due to terrorism. The human lives lost and the property destroyed constitute the direct costs, but it is the indirect costs – which far exceed, have a cascading effect, and are spread over a very wide area – that are troublesome.

358 Costs of private security measures apart, the time consumed in going through the security checks; the slowdown; the non-utilisation of men, establishment and machinery (or the idling) that such checks cause; and the fear and insecurity in the human mind which reduces its productivity, all cause immense loss. By reason of the 'insecurity', investment generally, and the economic cycle particularly, stand affected. In the competitive global market, the country loses out to those countries which are not targets of terrorism or which have been able to successfully protect themselves from its ill-effects.

359 Direct and indirect, the injury could be hundreds of thousands of crores of Rupees. Such being the extent of injury, the allocation of funds has to be accordingly approached. Unlike the expense on law & order, it is more akin to the expense on the defence of the nation.

360 The expenditure on fighting terrorism may not be as visible as other expenditure, for much of it will go into intelligence-gathering and processing as also for working out ways and means of combating it. However, if we assess the cost which the citizens and the nation have to bear because of terrorism, including social and opportunity costs, this expenditure will be only a small portion of the injury that will not occur (or get 'saved').[76] It will be more than justified.

361 Looked at differently, for the establishment and operations of the agencies and set-ups as herein envisaged, huge funds will be required. These funds will be less than what people and businesses will pay as insurance premium in the light of the happenings of the recent past. Of course, we may not ask a particular business house or establishment, which is vulnerable, to shell out extra funds towards government security agencies as compared to that which they otherwise do to an insurance company. But, in practical terms, one rupee as contribution to this effort will save five rupees as premium to the insurance company. Above all, it will prevent damage, and not merely compensate that which later occurs.

362 Once again, the fight against terrorism will need effort and expense where the bulk will be towards intelligence-gathering and prevention, and only a small amount will be towards making and updating laws, investigation, prosecution, courts and punishment, and of which, again, investigation will take the bulk. In the ultimate analysis, making available sufficient resources for establishing and operating such super fast-track courts will be more than reimbursed by a proportionate, reduced need for expenses on other security measures; the saving of opportunity costs will be a bonus.

363 The following table depicts the difference in 'distribution' of the effort and expense (of the notional 100 Rupees earmarked for each) between dealing with Crime (as traditionally or conventionally understood) on the one hand

---

76 a fair amount of which 'savings' will be recovered in routine as taxes by the State

and modern-day Terrorism on the other.[77]

		Crime	Terrorism
1.	Intelligence-gathering & processing	2	85
2.	Policing	25	10
3.	Investigations	30	3
4.	Courts	30	1.5
5.	Punishment and correction	13	0.5

It is this distribution that not only the policy-makers, but more importantly, the public and the taxpayers, need to understand and appreciate.

364 All this expenditure is certain to cost our country a great deal, but that is the price one has to pay to survive in the world of today; to grumble about it is no better than complaining about the expenditure on the locks that we have been putting on our doors, and which has become a way of life for us. Terrorism being a war by proxy, what is otherwise allocated as expenditure for the defence of the nation, in reality, falls under the same head; only the terminology is different and there is an overlap as well. In any case, for the security of the nation and its populace, increased expenditure ought to be a lesser concern.

12. Generally

365 Nearing the end of this topic, all that can be said is that a long battle is ahead of us where, alongside the conventional as well as the latest surveillance, both the executive branch and the statutory provisions of our justice system and administration need to gear up for the fight.

366 Over the last couple of years, the nature of the terrorist activities has undergone a transformation. The activities have turned more brutal than ever before, and the modus operandi has seen a drastic change. Today, the terrorist has become more sophisticated and knows how to attack in places where it hurts the most. Then why should our attitude remain the same? Democratic methods are useful against people who understand democracy, and not against those who have contempt for it.

367 One cannot fight an enemy as draconian as terrorism with laws and rules meant for the civilised. The requirement is of a quiver full of statutory measures of unprecedented scope and ones that not only match the weapons and tactics of the terrorists, but also carry sufficient punch to spare. It must not be forgotten that it is only by deploying methods

77 These figures are rough and ready, only to put the point across. The distribution as denoted by the figures in the last column when compared to the distribution as denoted by the figures for general crime in the third column is so different because terrorist acts are few, and it is the constant intelligence gathering and processing that requires funds. Further, the '100' as the notional total for each is, in actuality, less for terrorism than that it is for fighting general crime.

such as these that terrorism can be effectively dealt with. Otherwise, the Rule of law may fail and terrorism may come to rule.

368 To deal with terrorism, it will require innovative thinking; quick and bold decision-making; at times, risky (rescue or retaliatory) actions; and in the event of failure, exercise of restraint by the critics. There are also certain other thoughts and actions which the fight against terrorism will entail, but some of these, due to their nature, are best left unstated in a work like this, i.e. best left to be addressed by those who take up the task on behalf of the government and those who implement it. Alongside the field of policy and law, we have to act by ourselves in many a field, of which the most important is technology,[78] for as a sequel to a terrorist attack, international support is more as condolences than as action.

369 Unless we develop a highly efficient intelligence network to anticipate terror threats – (1) so that they can be neutralised in time and hopefully, the terrorists also caught; and (2) if we are unable to (i.e., they succeed), their orchestrators know that evidence against them is also there to justify retaliatory and other appropriate action – all laws for combating terrorism will be useless. In all probability, the damage would have been done and there will be nobody whom the system could arrest, charge, prosecute and punish.

370 Input from the police officers, intelligence officers and other officers in the field as to the measures required will need to be given greater weight and require quicker action. The government could galvanise specialists, serving or retired, to come up with a plan that produces the results that inspire public confidence. It is not that there is a lack of expertise; it is only commitment to the cause that is lacking.

371 There needs to be greater stress on issues like ensuring better community policing. While increase in strength and proficiency is generally called for, presently, on an average how many commandos and policemen guard a VVIP and how many in number (as also the standards in professionalism and equipment) is left to the typical citizen (as numbers per capita) is also a question to be considered. There is, in the final analysis, no substitute for efficient local policing. To that end, carrying out the much-needed police reforms must be given priority as a critical aspect of the fight against terrorism. Corruption in administration, governmental functioning and law enforcement is something which is a general problem across the board, but from the terrorism point of view also, it requires attention, for without that, terrorism would be difficult to control.

372 True, a typical citizen (common man) might think that except his personal safety, nothing else concerns him, and that it is only for the Government to do its task. Yet, if we have to fight this battle, at least the learned must

78 which is why encouragement of education, particularly technical education, is called for. See Topic 6 of Chapter 9 supra.

participate in the development of the thought process on how such 'safety' – of the nation as a whole – can, in practical terms, be achieved.

373 There are also more reasons, the primary being to understand the rationale behind the approach and thus overcome the proverbial opposition to change – be it qua the privilege against self-incrimination, or conviction on belief evidence, or the increased tolerance of the public to surveillance that impinges on individual privacy. To that extent, this topic (on Terrorism) addresses issues which at first blush may not appear to be law-related; nevertheless they constitute the very foundation for the law that we need. This explains both the inclusion in a work like this as also content that veers from the traditional.

374 In the context of developing laws and systems, it may be noted that after the 9/11 (11.09.2001) attacks on the World Trade Centre, the United States of America enacted (on 26.10.2001) a law, commonly known as the USA PATRIOT Act.[79] The statute gave unprecedented powers to law enforcement agencies in their fight against terrorism. Similarly, in England, there were the Terrorism Act, 2000; Anti-terrorism, Crime and Security Act, 2001; the Criminal Justice Act, 2003; and the Prevention of Terrorism Act, 2005. Finally, the Terrorism Act, 2006 (30.03.2006) gave a new definition to what would be offences relating to terrorism and also gave vast powers to the intelligence and enforcement agencies, or provided the tools required to tackle terrorism. Australia and other European countries have also framed tough laws. As the ensuing period has shown, it is measures as these that have proved effective, and we can usefully look into some of these.

375 Topic 2 of Chapter 9 supra, and Topics 13 and 14 of Chapter 13 infra, have argued for putting in place a central set-up for receiving comments, suggestions, thoughts, etc. from Judges, judicial officers, lawyers and the public. To put in place the right systems to make laws to tackle terrorism, including preventive systems, special emphasis on that will be required. Moreover, it will need to be a part of every police officer's implied statutory duty (whatever be his rank) or, in any case, his moral duty, to spare some time and effort to pen and send suggestions to the central set-up at least a few times a year. It is that collection of material which will help the lawmakers frame the finest laws.

376 Without adequate and effective laws, we will be unable to protect ourselves as a nation and as a society. It is not simply framing stringent laws, but also of skilfully framing them and implementing them in the right manner – eschewing misuse. Stated differently, the AT-laws are akin to a life-saving drug with many unavoidable side effects, which must be used only when absolutely necessary, and where nothing else will work – and used they have to be.

79 The contrived acronym stands for: Uniting and Strengthening America by Providing Appropriate Tools Required to Intercept and Obstruct Terrorism Act.

377 It is inevitable that laws and systems as these will impinge the citizens' right to privacy as part of their constitutional rights. This has been addressed in sub-topic 9 of Topic 7 (Liberty, Human Rights and Crime Control) at pp3~ supra. Suffice it to note that the victims of terrorism–of yesterday and those living under fear today – deserve that a more accurate 'balance' be arrived at.

378 The sovereignty and integrity of the nation have to be preserved at all cost. The security of the State and its citizens is of paramount importance. The individual's rights are subservient to the larger interests of society. If the prevailing circumstances in the country pose a threat to the nation's integrity and sovereignty, as they presently do, systems and laws of sufficient potency to prevent terrorism, and to protect citizens and their property, are essential.

379 In the past, anti-terrorism laws have been misused by the police to threaten and terrorise those fighting for economic and social justice, and have been applied to arrest people from all walks of life. Experience with TADA and POTA has shown many cases of persons being arrested wrongly and unnecessarily. Although many may not have been wholly innocent, they need not have been booked under the stringent laws. It is neither feasible nor proper to use the cannon ball (anti-terrorism laws) each time simply because the fly was suspected to be a wasp, or only because the typical house-fly could not be swatted. Such misuse renders the law ineffective, leaving it prone to public disapproval.

380 Finally, we must be alive to the difference between erroneous or unnecessary use of these systems, set-ups and laws on the one side and mischievous use on the other. Misuse of the intelligence agencies or the information collected, or of the investigation agencies, for political or other sinister purposes is a grave 'wrong'–perhaps no less than terrorism. It only saps the potency of the laws and systems that are in place to ensure the security of the State. The 'solution' lies not in the cold print of the statute book but in the integrity and conscience of those responsible.

381 Once again–like spanners of various sizes hanging from the hooks in the mechanic's workshop, or the pots & pans of various sizes in a modern kit-chen, or the medicines of varying potency (strength) for different diseases in the clinic–we need separate laws in the following order of potency:

(1) Anti-Terrorism;
(2) Anti-Drugs & Narcotics;
(3) against Organised Crime;
(4) to help maintain Public Order; and lastly
(5) the conventional penal laws–The Indian Penal Code and the very many special and local laws, and the like.

Alongside general reform in criminal procedures, each statute needs to have an inbuilt or companion procedural Codes – as offence-specific tailoring of procedures. A set of new laws as above (with some overlap) will help ensure the correct use of the right tool for the right occasion.

382 The statutory framework will accordingly provide the right set of tools to effectively counter terrorism. Thus, it is the special laws, surveillance, intelligence, investigation, prosecution and fast-track adjudication followed by deterrent punishment which can save the society from the scourge of terrorism. Unless the terrorist is given a clear message that our laws and systems will not lag behind, he will not hold back. It is that assessment of his which will cause a change in his thought process–something similar to the principle for general crime, which has been analysed in Topic 6 (sub-topic 3) at pp3~ supra.

383 To conclude, the discussion in this topic is intended to do no more than help spur new thinking by all concerned. Hopefully, such thinking will allow us as a nation to anticipate emerging trends and tactics in terrorism and bring to light the issues – understanding the terrorists' psychology; the basic policy; the role of intelligence, policing, investigation, prosecution, trials and punishment; and other related matters – that need to be considered in order to tackle terrorism. Understanding these issues at the analytical and policy levels will also help upgrade our anticipatory and pre-emptive operational capabilities to defeat the terrorist threat in all its current and future manifestations.

☆ ☆ ☆

-: End of Topic 10 :-

Chapter 10

Criminal Law and Procedures

Topic 14 Procedural Reform – General and offence-specific

Sub-topic 3 Offence-Specific Tailoring of Procedures

Chapter 10

Criminal Law and Procedures

Topic 14 Procedural Reform – General and offence-specific

Note: 'Dishonoured Cheques' is the subject discussed in sub-topic 3 of Topic 14 of Chapter 10 (Criminal Law and Procedures), which is titled 'Offence-Specific Tailoring of Procedures'. It takes a complaint case under Section 138 of the Negotiable Instruments Act for a dishonoured cheque as the basis for discussion, which begins from para 12 and continues till para 147. The remaining part of sub-topic 3 has not been excerpted. The discussion proceeds on certain assumptions which are not yet part of our procedural law. However, law reform being the objective, attending to these is but inevitable. A related issue – Using post-dated cheques as security – is addressed in Topic 8 of Chapter 8, which topic is part of the series (Topics 2 to 8) relating to Banking and Debt Recovery, and this has also been excerpted in the later part. The page headers have been suitably changed and the para numbers have also been changed to begin from 1.

3. Offence-Specific Tailoring of Procedures

1 Topic 14 seeks to expound a fundamental change in our approach towards criminal procedures. The proposed change comprises two parts: (1) reform in the basic procedures as the first step; and (2) thereafter, or as the second step, a still further change as suited to that offence. The current problem having been detailed in sub-topic 1 and the fundamental changes listed in sub-topic 2, this sub-topic 3 seeks to demonstrate the scope, rather the utility, of the second – offence-specific tailoring of procedures.

1. Generally

2 In our quest to put in place the best criminal justice system, the general reform in procedures[1] will have to be followed by further reform, depending on the type of offence that is in question. In practical terms, such further reform will involve keeping particular offences (or similar types of offences) in the forefront, and then seeking to review and amend the aforesaid basic/general procedures so as to carry out offence-specific tailoring of procedures, and, thus, achieve the highest possible levels of efficiency and accuracy, including prevention of delays.

3 The principle being expounded may be explained first. In a number of fields, we have a basic system or approach followed by a second stage

1 which will be done across all types of offences

where we identify the precise problem or the need, and then devise or evolve specific, at times innovative, methods, systems or procedures, which enable us to achieve the objective with greater efficiency and effectiveness. Descriptions like 'custom-built' or 'made-to-order' are used.[2]

4 One illustration would be of the special tools (spanners and wrenches) in a workshop, a particular one being used depending on the need.[3] Similarly, with computers, 'custom-made' or 'adapted' means a computer having modified or assembled hardware or software to suit the needs or preferences of the user. Here, 'customising' denotes putting together a computer facility catering to a specific customer's individual requirements.

5 Another illustration would be of doctors conducting pathological tests, including culture and sensitivity tests, before prescribing a particular drug/medication. This is why, in a typical chemist shop, we see not just one broad-spectrum antibiotic (and maybe a painkiller) to look after every ailment of the human body, but hundreds of different medications.[4] The same way, we need specifically designed procedures to detect, investigate, prosecute and adjudicate, for purposes of prevention and punishment, aberrations in human behaviour, which law defines as an offence.

6 As noted earlier, by and large, our criminal procedures were originally designed for trial before the jury and for offences which were primarily violent, though they were also extended to the trial of offences where no violence was involved. However, the last century (particularly the last two decades) has seen a substantial change. First, the jury system has long been abolished. Second, of all cases pending before criminal courts, those relating only to violence are no longer the bulk, but are only a small component. Third, even of those relating to violence (say, murder), the pattern of evidence is very different than that it was a century ago, and there is increased reliance upon documents, records and also forensics.

7 Procedural law – rather the approach to investigation and adjudication – cannot be either one-track or bound to rigid traditions. Our approach to-wards procedure must be one which permits its tailoring to the needs of the subject – as the discussion in this sub-topic demonstrates. We must not hesitate to evolve newer forms of procedure more suited to it (the particular offence) and then put in place such procedures which serve the purpose, so that justice is not only quick and effective, but also rendered at lower cost.

8 Earlier, the various sub-chapters of Chapter 7 had argued for general change in civil court procedures. Chapters 7-02 and 7-03 had in particular detailed how pre-trial procedures can help filter the rival claims and contentions. Thereafter, Chapter 8 had argued (for the second stage) a

2 i.e., according to the specifications of an individual user/purchaser or in accordance with particular instructions or requirements

3 See similar illustration in Topic 1 (paras 31 and 32) of Chapter 8 at pp3~ supra.

4 each designed and intended for a particular ailment

case for further tailoring and special designing of procedures so as to be suited to the particular litigation type. There is no reason why similar benefits cannot be obtained for most, if not all, criminal prosecutions.

9 Topic 2 of this Chapter 10 had pointed out the problem of White-collar crimes, and Topic 3 had argued a case for special procedures for investigating and prosecuting those crimes. Now, this Topic 14 argues a case for a general change in criminal procedures, including those for cases where violence or injury to human body is involved, while this sub-topic 3 in particular concentrates on the 'second stage' – of offence-specific tailoring – though that theme runs throughout the topic, rather the chapter. The attempt, once again, is to show: (1) the need for a basic change in the procedures (in the context of the present situation); (2) the concept of offence-specific tailoring of procedures; (3) the extent of change that is possible; (4) some thoughts on the frame of the Rules by which changes can be carried out; and (5) the benefits of doing so.

10 Accordingly, in this sub-topic 3, we take some samples to demonstrate and explain how such change – or the further 'tailoring' – can be effected. In the first part, we take up as the subject for study, complaints under Sections 138 and 142 of the Negotiable Instruments Act [26 of 1881], and examine how procedures therefor could be reformed to advantage. This runs into somewhat greater detail. Further, the discussion in the first part of this sub-topic wanders beyond criminal procedures into the general law regarding dishonour of cheques, but doing so was found necessary to enable better expression, as also for the sake of completeness. The later half (of this sub-topic) then makes short references to other subjects (offences) with a similar objective – to demonstrate how tailoring of procedures can help remove the present inefficiencies.

11 It may be clarified that though Computerisation of courts and use of technology as discussed in Chapter 13 infra is still to take place, we will, while giving some illustrations, particularly in the first half of this sub-topic, proceed on the assumption that Computerisation has been implemented.

2. Section 138 [Negotiable Instruments Act]

12 The Banking, Public Financial Institutions and Negotiable Instruments Laws (Amendment) Act [66 of 1988] inserted Chapter XVII comprising Sections 138 to 142 in the Negotiable Instruments Act, with effect from 1.04.1989. This was done with a view to enhance the acceptability / reliability of cheques in settlement of liabilities by holding the drawer criminally liable for a contractual breach in case of the bouncing of a cheque due to insufficiency of funds in the account or for the reason that it exceeds the arrangements made by the drawer. It also seeks to provide adequate safeguards to prevent harassment of honest drawers. The legislative purpose is to promote efficacy of banking and to ensure that in commercial or contractual transactions, cheques are not dishonoured and credibility in transacting business through cheques is

maintained.[5] The amendment was introduced to further a public policy to punish a special sort of commercial fraud. It was designed to prevent damage to trade, commerce and banking caused by worthless cheques.

13 This is a classic example of law reform, well intended, but failing to serve the purpose primarily for two reasons: (1) a wrong interpretation; and (2) following the traditional procedures without adaptation. The result has been both delays and injustice. There is no real relief. The first (erroneous interpretation) relates to inclusion of post-dated cheques within its ambit. There is a world of difference between situations where the cheque merely substitutes what could have been a cash payment on one side and where it operates merely as a security for a loan / credit taken to be paid for later or on a future date. To include post-dated cheques within the ambit of Section 138 is wrong.

14 A post-dated cheque is nothing more than a mere promise to discharge the present obligation on a future date, and failure to do so cannot be termed as a crime.[6] This aspect has been addressed in Topic 8 (sub-topic 3) of Chapter 8 [excerpted at pp120 infra] and suffice it is to re-emphasise it here. In any case, to punish a person for non-payment of a post-dated cheque is wrong. The drawer has to be equated with a debtor in civil courts or before the DRT, and not treated as an accused before a criminal court. Keeping aside that aspect, the discussion here is on an altogether different issue, i.e., on the desirability of evolving more efficient procedures for adjudication of complaints arising out of dishonoured cheques.

3: The Present Procedures

15 A complaint as this is essentially a private complaint under Section 200 Cr.P.C. If the Court, after going through the complaint and following the procedures prescribed by Section 200 [... shall examine upon oath the complainant and the witnesses present, if any ...] is satisfied that a case under Section 138 is made out,[7] it takes cognizance and issues process under Section 204 Cr.P.C – summons to the accused. Being a summons case under Chapter XX of the Code, proceedings under Section 251 are taken and particulars of the offence are recorded – charges are framed informally. See para 79 infra. The complainant's evidence, defence evidence, arguments followed by judgment and sentence, could – viewed

---

5 See *NEPC Micon Ltd vs Magma Leasing Ltd* 1999-4 SCC 253,'62 = AIR 1999 SC 1952.

6 An empirical survey will reveal that post-dated cheques comprise over 98% of the complaints filed, of which '95' were security for a debt. 2% may be a manipulation.

7 On this score, the 2002 amendment to the Negotiable Instruments Act gave relief by doing away with the need for pre-summoning evidence. Earlier, the practice was to follow the procedure prescribed by Section 200, where the complainant and witnesses were examined by the Court on oath before issuing process to the accused. After the 2002 Amendment, the Magistrate need not record this on oath. Now the complainant's affidavit in support of the complaint together with the affidavit of witnesses is taken as the basis by the Court. If the Court is satisfied, summons to the accused are issued.

as a ground reality – take up to five years. Is this not ineffective justice, or in any case delayed justice, for the holder of the cheque?

4. Some of the Problems faced

16 Let us then examine some of the problems being faced. First, primarily by reason of inclusion of post-dated cheques, which are a mere security for a loan advanced, the quantum of Section 138 complaints before Magistrates is simply huge. In some judicial districts, these may comprise almost 40% of the cases in number, though the time each case consumes is not as much as that consumed by other criminal cases. Further, in some judicial districts, because of the sheer volume of Section 138 complaints, the trial of such cases takes years, and only shows that law on this score has failed to serve the purpose.

17 The complaints as actually filed under Section 138 are sketchy and, at times, bereft of even the required particulars. This causes further problems as also delay. The accused too place false and fanciful defences, and deploy all kind of tactics to delay.

18 Unlike that for other forms of crime, the punishment here (in so far as the complainant is concerned) is not a means of seeking retribution, but is more a means to ensure payment of money. The complainant's interest lies primarily in recovering the money rather than seeing the drawer of the cheque in jail. The threat of jail is only a mode to ensure recovery. As against an accused who is willing to undergo a jail term, there is little available as remedy for the holder of the cheque.

19 If we were to examine the number of complaints filed which were 'compromised' or 'settled' before the final judgment on one side and the cases which proceeded to judgment and conviction on the other, we will find that the bulk was settled and only a minuscule number continued. See the table in Topic 8 (sub-topic 3) of Chapter 8 [excerpted at pp127 infra].

20 Further, of a notional 100 complaints that are filed, the claim for money (the post-dated question apart) is genuine in 97, and it is only in 3 that the claim is either non-existent or inflated. Of these (the first 97), 90 are settled, i.e., the money is paid back, and in the remaining seven, the drawer of the cheque has no money and cannot arrange any. Of these seven, at least six could undergo a jail term, though in five out of these six, the complainant himself, on humanitarian considerations, and once satisfied that the accused has no assets or was initially not a cheat, does not press for a jail term.

21 Thus, in the strict meaning of the term, it is less of an offence against society which ought to be tried by the criminal courts, and more of being only a means or method of ensuring return of money. Here too, dishonour of a cheque which was to be paid *in presenti* is an offence in which society has an interest, but a jail term for dishonour of a post-dated cheque is something which societal interest and public policy

deprecate. A distinction between the two and confining the criminal procedures to the first is called for. See para 112 infra.

22 So far, it was about the difficulties of a holder of a cheque (or the complainant). Even the accused (drawer) has to face certain difficulties, many of which are avoidable and some of which are, in fact, not fair. A few of these are addressed in paras 130 to 132 infra. Some difficulties in this regard are also discussed in Topic 8 of Chapter 8 supra.

23 Despite the fact that a cheque may not always be for good or subsisting consideration, in actual practice, questions of absent consideration (for the cheque) have little bearing. Cheques are often signed or given in blank for convenience and/or in good faith. Take the case of a person (A) who gives another person (B) a blank 'Account Payee' cheque for purchase of a property, but the recipient (B), instead of purchasing the property for A, fills-in (writes) his confidant's (C's) name and then presents it in clearing. Upon 'Stop payment', C issues a notice, which is followed by a criminal complaint.

24 Though not common, one does see businessmen carrying half a dozen cheque books (of others) in their briefcase with cheques signed in blank. Now, if this briefcase were stolen and the cheques misused, both the drawer and the carrier have only to thank themselves and not find fault with the laws and the justice system. People must be educated not to issue blank cheques,[8] even if the person they are entrusting them with is not dishonest, for they may be stolen or lost from his custody.

25 Similarly, one cannot go to a home appliances store; order a refrigerator; pay for it by cheque; and instead of the delivery van unloading the refrigerator, see the postman deliver an envelope containing a notice under Section 138 read with Section 142. There can be scores of such misuse.

26 Cheques are sometimes issued as a result of coercion, deception, trick, or fraud; they may have forged signatures, altered amounts, and the like. There can be a number of situations where the cheque is not really for good consideration (in the sense that consideration has not passed or was unlawful) or consideration has ceased to exist (in the sense that there has been a subsequent failure of consideration, or a payment or adjustment). The complaint, therefore, is not backed by honest consideration. The problem here is that once a complaint is made, the accused has no real say except create obstruction or cause delays. At times, the attitude of the courts is very inflexible. They can even be heard to say (metaphorically):

> Is this a cheque from the cheque book issued by the bank to you? If you cannot deny that, bring the money or go to jail. We will hear nothing else.

A stance as this maybe failure of justice, though only in a few cases.

---

8 It will be worthwhile to print a small informative leaflet on the consequences of cheque dishonour and the care to be taken in regard to the use of cheques. Banks must issue this booklet as a part of every cheque book, or once a year, to the account holder.

27 In these complaint cases, on the issues of fair trial, adducing evidence for the accused; issuing of cheques as a security; and ingredients of legally enforceable debt, of late, some welcome notes have been sounded.[9] Even on the issue of compensation and not a jail term, in *P. Suresh Kumar vs R. Shankar*,[10] there has been a move towards the right approach. On this issue (fine and compensation), useful observations are to be found in *Dilip S. Dahanukar vs Kotak Mahindra Co. Ltd.*[11]

28 Recently, in *Krishna Janardhan Bhat vs Dattatraya G Hegde*,[12] the Supreme Court observed that courts must take into account the ground realities while deciding the cheque-bouncing cases. It was noted that:

> The courts must be on guard to see that merely on the application of presumption, as contemplated under Section 139 of the Negotiable Instruments Act, the same may not lead to injustice or mistaken conviction.
>
> Other important principles of legal jurisprudence, namely presumption of innocence as human rights and the doctrine of reverse burden introduced by Section 139 should be delicately balanced. Such balancing acts, indisputably would largely depend upon the factual matrix of each case, the materials brought on record and having regard to legal principles governing the same.

The Court also reviewed the recent case law on the subject and gave guidelines regarding application of reverse burden of proof in such cases.

29 A word of caution. Of the complaints filed, if we exclude those relating to post-dated cheques as security, the claim is genuine in 97%. Yet if we talk of law, procedures and trial, there needs to be some methodology by which a genuine defence (in that odd case or the 3%) does get a hearing, while the ability to conjure up a defence to the genuine claim (in 97%) does not delay the process.

30 It may be noted that as a ground reality, of the cheques written out, far more than the 3% cheques referred to above are without consideration and, on their face, are completely valid for a Section 138 complaint. However, for reasons of honesty and morality, the holder does not use them to file a complaint. Even in the 3% as aforesaid, it is only in 1% that the complainant is positively dishonest; in the rest, the drawer could also be partly, if not wholly, in the wrong, and the complainant is using the procedures only to exert pressure and bring about a settlement of what he thinks is his just claim.

---

9 *T. Nagappa vs Y.R. Muralidhar* 2008-5 SCC 633 = 2008-6 JT 153 = 2008-6 SCALE 642; *Sudhir Kumar Bhalla vs Jagdish Chand* 2008-7 SCC 137 = 2008-6 JT 549 = 2008-6 SCALE 626; and *Lalit Kumar Sharma vs State of U.P.* 2008-5 SCC 638 = 2008-7 SCALE 778

10 2007-4 SCC 752 = AIR 2007 SC 1774

11 2007-6 SCC 528,'42 = JT 2007-6 SC 204 = 2007-5 SCALE 452

12 2008-4 SCC 54 = JT 2008-1 SC 485 = 2008-1 SCALE 421

31 True, if the cheque has been obtained by playing a trick or fraud, or consideration is absent, a complaint cannot be allowed to succeed; yet, a plea of fraud or failed consideration ought not to be available to every drawer of a cheque (i.e. an accused) in order to delay the proceedings. A balance has to be struck. The Court may even consider directing the deposit of money and payment thereof to the payee of the cheque, subject to return if the matter is adjudicated against the holder of the cheque (original complainant) in a civil court. It will, of course, have to be a civil suit of a special type.

32 In any case, the 'defence' of the accused should not be looked at with disdain. Instead, if it is more than plausible – which on occasions, though very few, it is – the Court should go into the matter and not 'reject' it without even giving it a look. A false defence, like a false complaint, should, nevertheless, constitute a separate offence. The endeavour of procedural law is to prevent false defences as also false complaints.

33 More importantly, though a person may be held guilty and sentenced to a fine and/or imprisonment, there is no provision for passing a (executable) Decree / Order for recovery of the money. True, as punishment for the offence, apart from imprisonment, the fine may extend to 'twice' the amount of the cheque, but that fine goes to the State.[13] What is also required is a mechanism other than a jail term which enables recovery of the money. See para 123 infra.

34 The amount of the cheque apart, the question of interest – at market rate and with quarterly rests from the date appearing on the cheque till actual payment – is another issue which the statute does not address. See para 124 infra. There are several other incongruities and not so fair manifestations of law on this score, but since this topic is confined to criminal procedures, those (other such) problems are not discussed here.

35 By a special amendment [Act 55 of 2002], the traditional recording of evidence of the complainant and witnesses (like bankers) before summoning the accused has been dispensed with. See Sections 143 to 147. Although a welcome move, this has been only a partial remedy. It needs and calls for a complete change in the systems and working procedures.

5. Some thoughts towards reform

36 If one were to do away with the traditional criminal procedures and seek to evolve offence-specific procedures for complaints under Section 138 of the Negotiable Instruments Act, it would add to the efficacy. And alongside such procedures, if there were: (1) availability of sufficient number of courts with support infrastructure; (2) computerisation along with Case

---

13 See Section 138 and the first proviso to Section 143(1). Since the power of the Magistrate to levy fine payable to the State is limited by Section 29(2) Cr.P.C., the amount is usually given to the complainant as compensation as per Section 357. See para 27 supra. Amendment of this provision is however necessary. A greater amount must go to the State as a fine.

and litigation Management; and (3) whittling down the privilege against self-incrimination, it would further add to the efficiencies.

37 Some of the following could be considered for being incorporated as part of the procedures for the trial of a Section 138 complaint:

.1 Prescribed Form for a Complaint together with a questionnaire, documents, and an Affidavit (also in a prescribed form) in support.

.2 The personal presence of the complainant on every date, when he is represented through counsel, be dispensed with as it is more of a harassment to the complainant than to the accused.

.3 A written response on Affidavit be required (by the Summons) from the accused, putting forward the defences he has to offer. As part of the response to the complaint, the accused should be required to produce documents, answer interrogatories, which the rules and the practice directions may specify, and also state whether the accused is willing to suffer a Decree executable by the civil court for recovery of the amount.

.4 Once such a reply has been received (or an opportunity therefor given), opportunity to the complainant to file a rejoinder or further affidavit of evidence be given. The necessary 'certificates' and 'statements' can be sent for directly from the bank.

.5 The formalities of appearance, bail, discharge[14] or charge, and a direction as to how much evidence is necessary, if at all, can be carried out in a single hearing (that very hearing or the next). There could even be an Order for recovery of money, discharge, or an Order dispensing with the trial.

.6 Trial procedures can be shortened.

.7 Also required along with the judgment is an Order (or a Decree) for recovery of that amount with interest, executable by the principal court of civil jurisdiction.

.8 Interest and costs can be awarded; a fine can be levied; and payment in instalments can also be considered.

.9 While imposing the sentence of imprisonment / fine as provided by Section 138, the Court may take into consideration whether the payment has been made voluntarily and if so, at what point of time, and whether it has been made with or without interest. Further, for those who pay within a reasonable time or for those whose default is not mischievous, the sentence of imprisonment should not be imposed except in rare cases.

.10 For the purposes of limitation for filing a civil suit based upon the dishonoured cheque, the period between the date of service of the summons of the complaint under Section 138 till its final disposal or

---

14 on the analogy of Section 245(2) Cr.P.C. However, in view of the decision in *Adalat Prasad v Rooplal Jindal* 2004-7 SCC 338 = 2004-7 SCALE 137 = JT 2004-7 SC 243, to do so, a statutory amendment will be necessary – as part of tailoring the procedures for dishonoured cheques.

one year, whichever is less, may be considered for being excluded, but such exclusion should be only for the purposes of a claim on the cheque as distinct from that on the original debt.

If procedure on these lines are made part of the law, it will make the process effective and quick, and will also help remove delays.

38 Though relating more to Case and litigation Management, a basic postulate is having courts which are insulated from overload. The Court's listing be within optimal limits and with no 'overloading' as that heavily tells upon the efficiency curve. It is to say that only that many cases be listed before a particular Magistrate (whether under the current or new procedures) as he can comfortably handle and give the requisite attention to each. Today, with over 50 cases on board, a Magistrate is badly overloaded, although his list ought not to exceed 20, or at most, 25.

39 With such reform in procedures – together with Case and litigation Management, Computerisation, as also adequate support infrastructure – there is no reason why that optimal cannot become something like '70' cases. But, be it 40, 70 or 100, the optimal limit should not be crossed. Then alone can they be classed as 'fast-track courts'.[15]

40 Another important issue to be addressed, and at this stage itself, is the 'cost of court time'. Despite its value being what it is[16] – and processing and trying one complaint may consume 10 hours or more of court and related time – the Rules prescribe a standard court-fee of Rs. 1.25 for a complaint. There are thousands of such complaints filed and they are only a drain on the criminal court's resources. A fair chunk of the complaints, in fact most, are filed by banks and finance companies.

41 For a complaint of this nature (as with many other crimes in today's scenario), the complainant must be charged with the cost of investigation, inquiry, prosecution and trial in the form of some reasonable amount to be paid as court-fee at the time of filing. The amount thereof be multi-tier, i.e., there should be three broad scales (percentage rates) with a minimum amount and also a maximum amount. An additional sum be made payable at a later date, depending on the court time actually consumed.

42 The burden of all these costs to the court (or court-fees) together with interest thereon ought to be ultimately shifted (in case of conviction) to the accused who allowed his cheque to be dishonoured, and made payable to the complainant, or (in case of acquittal) shifted to the complainant for having come forward with a false complaint. If there be a settlement between the two, then such costs must be recovered from both, leaving the question of apportionment amongst them as a part of the settlement, but to the court they remain liable jointly and severally.

---

15 See the discussion on fast-track courts in Topic 3 of Chapter 12 infra.

16 Presently, at least Rs. 2,000 per hour. See pp301 supra.

43 In other words, recovery of the costs of the court time consumed by reason of impropriety in conduct before it (the Court) – be it of the complainant or of the accused – ought to be the rule. The funds so generated can be used to establish and operate sufficient number of courts with modern & efficient support infrastructure, so that for a complaint under Section 138, the 'waiting time' is nil and even the processing time is as little as it could be.[17]

6. Detailing the Procedures further

44 Having listed the points, and proceeding on the premiss that the new Rules, Case and litigation Management systems, Computerisation, and sufficient number of Magistrates and support infrastructure as envisaged are all in place, we may now seek to detail some thoughts towards 'offence-specific' reform for Section 138 complaint procedures.

Complaint

45 We begin with the complaint, which, as noted earlier, is today bereft of particulars, lacking clarity and often confusing. The power of the Form[18] can be harnessed to help remove this deficiency and otherwise help 'speed up' the process. The Form for filing the complaint could be something like that below:

IN THE COURT OF THE Designation MAGISTRATE District

Court Code

Case Number

Date of filing 200

Full name of the complainant Father's name

Photograph of the complainant
If a corporate body, registration number

Address residence workplace

Bankers of the complainant their 9-digit code

versus or against

Full name of the accused Father's name

Photograph of the accused, if available

Address residence workplace

Police District/Station

where the accused resides where the accused's bank is situated

Complaint under Sections 138 and 142 of the Negotiable Instruments Act read with Section 200 of the Cr.P.C.

Sir,

I name of the complainant submit this complaint. The particulars of the cheque are:

17 See the discussion on waiting time in para~ of sub-topic 1 at pp3~ supra. See also Topic 2 (paras 30 to 44) of Chapter 14 which notes that a typical party (in the right) would be willing to pay additional court-fees (to cover such costs) if he is assured that there will be no waiting time.

18 discussed in detail in Topic 9 of Chapter 13 infra

Cheque No.	9-digit bank code	Amount figures	words	Date of cheque	Date of dishonour

Photocopies of the cheque, the return memo and the proof of despatch of the notice demanding payment appear on the reverse. Copies are also Annexures ...

Consideration: State in not more than fifty words the consideration for the cheque. Read the Rules in this regard, which also contain many specimens that give a cue. Attach photocopies of any documents as proof of consideration (maximum 5 sheets).

Interest: Does the amount of the cheque include interest? If it does, give the break-up of the principal and the interest and also specify the interest rate. Please calculate the interest commencing from the date of the cheque till the date of this complaint, and write the amount and the rate.

Date on which the cheque was delivered. If not known, the approximate month be stated.

Dishonoured for the reason ...... copy from the bank's return memo

If persons other than the signatory to the cheque are accused, please write "YES" and attach a sheet stating the facts and the grounds why they are also liable as accused.

Notice dated ......·......200... demanding payment sent vide Postal Receipt No. ... dated ......·......200 ... of Post Office city . Copy of the notice is Annexure .....

Response: If any has been received, give date in the right column and annex photocopy. If not, write 'NONE'. Also annex photocopy of any communication from the accused after delivery of the cheque till date in relation to the cheque.

Payment: If any has been received, give details. If no payment has been received, write 'NONE'.

Any other debt owed by the accused to the complainant: Give details. If none, write 'NONE'.

Security: If the complainant is holding any security for or in relation to the amount of the cheque, write 'YES' and give details of such security and its present-day value in an Annexure hereto.

Prayer: The present complaint be registered and action be initiated against the accused under Sections 138 and 142 of the Negotiable Instruments Act, 1881 and the accused be punished in accordance with law for the offence committed by him.

......·......200 ...

Complainant's full name in own handwriting Complainant's signature

If signing on behalf of a company/entity, write its full name also, affix rubber stamp and attach copy of the authority letter/resolution (duly certified as true).

e-bin, *e*-mail, and/or the mobile phone number to which communication/SMS may be sent

Certificate and verification: I, ... full name ... , having examined all relevant aspects, including documents & records, say that the contents of the above complaint are correct. I further say that there is neither any false averment nor concealment of anything material (facts, document or record). The Annexures hereto (total ..... pages) are true copies of the originals. I certify that the cheque was for consideration as detailed above and that the obligation of the accused to pay that still subsists. Having read and understood the requirement of Rule ... of the ... ... Rules as also all its implications and consequences, I append this Certificate to the above complaint comprising ..... pages and ... pages as annexures, each of which has been signed by me. My Affidavit in support is also attached.

Space for office stamp Complainant's signature

46 The specimen Form as aforesaid does not contain any column numbers. The final Form as prescribed will contain column numbers and with reference to each column, there will be instruction notes – quite like those with an application for issue of a passport prescribed by the Rules under the Passport Act. Some of the material from the aforesaid specimen Form could be shifted to the accompanying sheet.

47 The instruction notes could be something on these lines:

Please read the Rules & Guidelines (Publication No. ....). Before beginning to actually fill-up the Form for the complaint, you are advised to make a List of Events and collect all documents.

Hereafter the instruction notes may proceed item-wise (with reference to each column number of the prescribed Form) giving guidance on how it should be filled up along with samples or options to choose from.

Read the sample interrogatories as prescribed by Rule No. ... and keeping in view the facts of your case, you may add up to four more interrogatories in terms of the Rule.

If the cheque is signed by one person on behalf of another, including a corporate entity, then please state in respect of each accused, how and why they are liable.

If there are accused other than the signatory to the cheque, then attach a sheet detailing the name of the bank account holder, particulars (names and addresses) of the other accused and the basis on which they are sought to be made liable. Attach photocopies of supporting documents.

If there are more cheques than one, provided they are on the same bank account and by the same drawer, then an additional sheet be used for that column and photocopies be attached. For each such cheque, the consideration be separately stated.

Please double check the complaint as filled-in and the annexures as prepared so as to ensure 'zero-error' since any wrong statement is liable to penalties which may be severe.

Make an accurate and descriptive list of all annexures duly 'page numbered' and 'annexure numbered' [A, B, C and so on] and file it as an index to the complaint.

Use the prescribed rubber stamp for authentication. Please keep the originals carefully as your undertaking to produce them at the trial is, by the Rules, implicit.

(*Once it is complete*) You are advised that your complaint must state the truth and not sway therefrom. The consideration for the cheque must be good and subsisting. No material fact or document ought to be concealed. In this regard, you should Stop and think carefully before appending your signatures to the verification.

Having so done, you may append your signatures in permanent blue-black ink on every page of the original before filing it in court. Also sign the photocopies of annexures in token of their being true. The affidavit in support must be attested before a Notary specially notified for such complaints. Make as many copies as there are accused, and also retain extra photocopies with yourself.

After the basic Rules and Forms have been developed, instruction notes (on these lines) can be prepared and published. Column / Field numbers will make the use of Forms more convenient. See also para 137 infra.

48 To reiterate the essentials, a complaint must state (in anything from 20 to 50 words) the precise consideration for which the cheque was issued and received. Further, till the post-dated question is sorted out, the complaint must state the approximate date on which it was signed and delivered; a statement to the effect that the consideration therefor is good and valid, and subsists, i.e., the cheque has not been discharged in any way; (for partial payments) whether there are any other cheques of the accused with the complainant, and if so, their date, number and amount in a tabular form, along with other averments.

49 The complaint must be under the penalty of perjury, i.e., if any averment therein is found to be false or a relevant fact / document concealed, appropriate penalties can be imposed. To facilitate this, the certificate-cum-verification at the foot should be covered by a statutory definition that enables prosecution for any false statement / concealment.[19] There should also be a prescribed Form for an affidavit in support. The affidavit will re-verify the contents of the complaint, including the certificate at the bottom thereof as also the annexures, and being on 'Oath', it would then comprise 'evidence' in the technical sense.

50 A provision as this would deter people from filing false complaints and also prevent a number of mischiefs which complainants (as holders of dishonoured cheques) play. In all such cases, the Court should not hesitate in taking action – prosecuting the complainant for Perjury and / or Abuse of Process.

51 The Rules also need to provide for 'working' on self-attested photocopies. Presently, original cheques simply tagged to the file tend to get mutilated or even lost. The right form would be to work on photocopies while the original is placed in safe custody, to be sent for only in the case of need.

52 The Complaint Form can be in both print and electronic form. The Form for the complaint could be developed in a computer-compatible and user-friendly pattern. The information contained therein could then be lifted /

19 See the form for a Certificate at pp648 supra. See also the discussion on the need to Stop, think and double-check, before moving, in Chapter 11 infra.

keyed into the Court's computer and then either automatically or manually (as copy on and paste) 'lifted' for use for further proceedings. The specimen Form for the complaint given at pp95 supra can be designed in a computer-compatible form. An electronic Form (See Topic 10 of Chapter 13 infra) followed by laser printouts can work wonders in speeding up this part of criminal courts' work. It will not be long before interactive electronic forms will enable preparation and filing of the complaint.

53 To process the electronic forms, a computerised filing counter will be required. Alongside that could be a sufficiently large room with several counters where lawyers could bring their papers or soft copies and (for a fee) have them converted into the Courts' electronic filing format. The cheques, annexures, etc., can be scanned, digitised and stored. There will also be a special Notary here to attest before the necessary 'filing' (paper along with electronic copy) is done.[20]

Issuing the Process

54 Once a complaint in this form is received, the filing number and case number can be allotted. After initial scrutiny[21] (equivalent of taking cognizance under Sections 190 or 200 Cr.P.C.), the Process – in terms of Section 204 – can be issued to the respondent-accused the next day. As the contents of the complaint are on affidavit, pre-summoning evidence under Section 200 can be dispensed with. See also paras 83 - 86 infra. Today, with computers in operation, the 'Issuing of process', which took months (or till 2002, even years), can be completed within a day or two, or at the most three, i.e., the necessary groundwork is done by the registry whereafter the orders are passed by the Magistrate.

Summons

55 The issue of process having been ordered, the next step is preparing the summons. Here, instead of the traditional summons to the accused by the criminal court (in Form No.1 of the Second Schedule, which will apply even to a private complaint based on injury by use of sharp-edged weapon) the summons can be in a completely different and special form. It is not just serving the summons, but serving them in a form and manner that prevents, at least, one or two adjournments, or other delays.

56 The summons must include the details of the cheque: Bank name, Bank code, date, amount, name of the drawer, account number, and the date of dishonour. It will only be filling-up the blanks in a printed form. The summons ought to include a copy of the complaint (affidavit), photocopy of the cheque (or simply, the complete set of papers) and also require the accused to file in Court within two weeks of the receipt of summons,[22] an

20 Hopefully, a system of receiving the main complaint in an electronic form and then transferring it to the court's computer can be put in place. All it requires is a kind of a job work computer on the side of the filing computer which can do the needful, and then have both the paper and the electronic filing side by side. See further discussion on *e*-filing in Topic 5 of Chapter 13 infra.

21 Senior staff can carry out the necessary scrutiny and the Magistrate can scan through their report before passing the formal Orders.

22 or even merely give him an opportunity to do so

affidavit stating whatever he has to say in relation to the complaint and the cheque in question with sufficient details, and also answer the interrogatories. See para 63 infra. The summons will also contain reference to the Rules and the publications containing guidelines to respond. After all, the purpose of law is to do justice and not merely penalise.

57 A sample of the proposed Form for Summons to the Accused is as under:

IN THE COURT OF THE Designation MAGISTRATE District

| | | | | | | | | | | | | | | | | | | | |

Court Code Case Number

Cause title

Name and address of the accused
both residence and workplace

Summons to the Accused
on a complaint based upon a dishonoured cheque

WHEREAS a complaint under Section 138 of the Negotiable Instruments Act has been received from name of the Complainant in relation to Cheque No. .... dated ....200 ... for Rs. .... drawn on .... Bank.

You name of the Accused are hereby summoned to appear before this court on ....200 ... (...... day) at 10.00 A.M. (stagger time as per cause list)

Enclosed is a complete set of papers comprising a total of .... sheets.

Within two weeks of the receipt of these summons, you are required to file a Response in Form No. .... under Rule ... of .... Rules. The interrogatories provided by Rule ... may be answered.

Before filing your response, you are advised to carefully read the instruction notes and guidelines (Booklet No. .... available with the law book sellers). An advance copy of your response should be served upon the complainant or his Advocate. Failure to file a response or filing an incomplete response would enable the Court to draw such inference as it deems proper.

Make a note in your diary/calendar of the date '..... . ...200 ...', for if you fail to appear, warrants for arrest shall issue to ensure your presence. On that date, you are also required to submit a bail bond along with surety, which you may please keep ready.

You are also required to bring to the court the original Memo of your cheque book from which the aforesaid cheque was issued, the statement of account/pass book for the period one week before and one week after the issue of the cheque and also for the week after the alleged date of dishonour. Also bring with you photocopies of the aforesaid as the originals will be examined and returned, while copies will be retained on record.

In case you wish to concede your liability and request to pay in instalments, you may move an application along with any security in Form No. .... per Rule .... You may read Rule .... which gives guidelines for considering leniency in sentencing where liability is conceded on the first date itself and thereafter the payment together with costs, etc. is actually made within the time allowed.

GIVEN UNDER MY HAND AND THE SEAL OF THIS COURT on this .... day of .... 200 ... .

Seal Sd/-

Name of the Presiding Officer, the courtroom number, and the address of the court is noted here as part of the computer printout or by a clear synthetic rubber stamp.

58 The process of preparing the summons can be also 'computerised', i.e., the summons can be computer generated with the necessary details being 'lifted' by the computer from the complaint and placed here. Laser prints can be taken out and the seal of the Court and signatures of the official can be appended thereon. Electronic copies can be sent by *e*-mail to the complainant's lawyer and also (as advance copy) to the Process-Serving Establishment.

59 Summons issued, the next step is of serving them. Presently, serving summons upon the accused takes months; with a mischievous accused, it could take even years. The Registered Post AD service of summons often returns without service or proper acknowledgment. At the same time, the provisions of Section 144(2) are rather harsh and capable of misuse. Instead, it will be better to issue bailable (or even non-bailable) warrants and ensure his personal presence before the Court, rather than proceed to decide a criminal charge on the basis of 'deemed service'.

60 If a system for serving of process on the lines discussed in Topic 5 of Chapter 7-11 at pp1863 supra could be put in place, it will solve much of the problem. Such summons can be served within ten days of the issue, wherefore the date fixed should be about 30 days hence. Further, upon the summons being returned as 'served', the Court's computer can automatically send an *e*-mail or SMS to the complainant's lawyer, and if no such intimation is received, it would be for him (the lawyer) to get fresh summons issued and served before the date fixed.

61 If despite all this effort, service is not completed by the date fixed, the Court would not only issue fresh summons, but also direct the bank on which the cheque was drawn to furnish details of all known addresses so as to facilitate service of summons. It may even issue bailable (or even non-bailable) warrants to be executed by the local Police Station.

Response & interrogatories

62 Service of the Court's process upon the accused having been completed, the traditional criminal procedures do not provide for any response from the accused, but only for his physical appearance before the Magistrate

followed by supply of copies. In practical terms, it is not his '*Darshan*' (mere appearance) but a response to the complaint that is required. A response, if received in a prescribed form, can cut short so much of what is today the unnecessary 'trial work'. This is particularly where the discussion in this topic proceeds to what has been termed at the outset as 'further tailoring of the procedures, keeping in view the specific subject' so as to bring about efficiencies. As already noted, the law here needs to provide that failure to respond to the summons will have its consequences.

63 A few thoughts on the response. The response should require answers to three interrogatories, which may be prescribed by the Rules. Samples for these interrogatories are:

i Whether the cheque/s mentioned in the complaint was issued/signed/executed by the accused?

ii The precise reasons according to him (the accused):

a) Why was the cheque issued?

b) Why was the cheque (allowed to be) dishonoured?

c) Why was the dishonoured cheque not replaced by a bank's Pay Order immediately?

iii Whether the accused is willing to make payment and/or suffer a Decree (executable by the civil court) for recovery of the amount?

The aforesaid three should ordinarily cover the possible controversy. The complainant may add up to four more interrogatories by way of an application, which, upon an order of the Court, can be included with the summons, or later on, an opportunity to answer be given to the accused.

64 It may nevertheless be noted that the process of additional interrogatories will not be feasible to begin with because the concept (also discussed in Topic 7 of Chapter 7-02 at pp851 supra), despite its utility, is not common with the lawyers, and so for no explicable reason. Second, it will need application of mind by the Magistrate before permitting interrogatories at this stage. However, if a complaint is in the Form as proposed above and the Rules require a meaningful reply, further interrogatories may not be necessary at all.

65 The Rules (relating to a response) would advise the filing of an item/column-wise answer. It will give an opportunity to place a written statement of fact (version of the accused) detailing the circumstances in which the subject cheque/s came to be issued, the reasons for non-payment and the action taken by the accused (as the drawer of the cheque) thereafter. It may include a positive averment about receipt of the notice and such other facts which may go to show that no offence has been committed. The response may answer the interrogatories. Specimen Forms for the response can also be provided by the Rules.

66 In any case, the Rules and the prescribed Form will (along with other guidance notes) list the points/material which needs to be responded to

or explained. All relevant documents may be discovered and produced by the accused (copies attached). The accused be also given an opportunity to attach with the reply a true photocopy of the bank passbook or statement of account for the period commencing three days prior to the date of the cheque and till seven days after the dishonour complained of. Even the accused may include up to five interrogatories (as a part of his response) to be answered by the complainant.[23] The response may be received in both printed and electronic form.

67 True, critics might claim that some of the proposals will run foul of Article 20(3) of the Constitution,[24] but that is not so, for it is only giving an 'opportunity' and then, depending on the response (or failure of the response), raising an appropriate inference before returning a finding of fact. Asking for a response from the drawer of the cheque – as distinct from a man accused of murder in the Central Market – on a fair reading of the Constitutional provision (as it stands) is very much permissible. However, keeping aside that issue for the time being, as reform therein is also being separately argued for, it is procedures as these which we need, and it is these which would serve the intended purpose.

68 There is another way of looking at it, and it is that for what is 'appearing in evidence' against the accused, Section 313 Cr.P.C. provides that an 'opportunity' be given to the accused to explain. See para 87 infra. True, in practice, it is given after the close of the prosecution evidence, but there is no embargo or bar as to the stage. In a complaint case like this, such 'evidence' 'appears' at the initial stage itself – by production of the dishonoured cheque and the presumptions that attach – wherefore, no fault can be found in seeking a 'Response' from the accused.

69 In any case, an opportunity to file the answer as aforesaid must be given. If no answer is submitted within the time allowed or within the extended time, or if the answer is vague, improper, or otherwise insufficient, the Court may raise appropriate inferences. If, however, an answer is given, the Court would, at least, look at the answer and then decide how to proceed and what orders to pass.

70 A practical issue is authentication of the photocopies filed as documents with the complaint or response. A specific Rule should prescribe the rubber stamp[25] and also provide that the photocopies be attested by the

---

23 A written response to the complaint as also an answer to the four interrogatories may appear to be a duplication, but is necessary so as to prevent a party from avoiding to answer and also enable the Magistrate to seek the answers (if any) to the three basic questions. It may be noted that 'reply before the date fixed' will have its teething problems.

24 Topic 8 has addressed the issue of whittling down the privilege against self-incrimination. Prior thereto, Topic 7 (sub-topic 5) addressed the issue of presumption of innocence against the accused and how it could be correctly applied.

25 the modern synthetic rubber variety, which leaves a clear impression and in a particular colour. See the discussion on authentication of photocopies in ~~.

party by signing within the rubber stamp. This will ensure that the incidence of fake / manipulated photocopies is prevented and in case of breach, adjudication of the wrong can be readily carried out and the punishment inflicted. See para~ of Topic 2 (Perjury) of Chapter 11 infra.

Certificate from the Bank

71 Rules will also need to provide for receiving documents, copies, statements, certificates, etc., from the bankers of the accused as also from any other party, at the pre-trial stage. The oral evidence of the witnesses with original records can then be confined to rare occasions. See also the discussion on this in Topic 4 of Chapter 7-02 at pp786 *et seq*.

72 Inasmuch as banking operations are now almost electronic, Summons (to send a Certificate) can be sent by the Court to the concerned Bank (on which the cheque was drawn) by *e*-mail.[26] A Form for such Summons will need to be prescribed. The following is a sample:

IN THE COURT OF THE Designation MAGISTRATE District

Court Code

Case Number

Cause title

Summons to the Bank (name of the bank)
in relation to a complaint based upon a dishonoured cheque

The nine digit bank code may be noted here

WHEREAS a complaint under Section 138 of the Negotiable Instruments Act has been received from name of the Complainant in relation to Cheque No. .... nine digit bank code dated ......·.......200 ... for Rs. .... drawn on your bank, by (name of the accused) in relation to Account No (as appearing on the cheque) and said to have been dishonoured by you on ......·.......200 ... .

You name of the bank are hereby summoned to send to this court by *e*-mail, and failing that, on paper, a Certificate in form No (see sample in the next para) as provided by the Rules within the next seven days. If you fail to do so, the court may take coercive action. The case comes up before this court on ......·.......200 ... (....... day) at 10.00 A.M.

GIVEN UNDER MY HAND AND THE SEAL OF THIS COURT on this .... day of .... 200 ....

Seal Sd/-

Name of the Presiding Officer, the courtroom number, and the address of the court as also the *e*-mail address

73 There is also need to prescribe a Form for the 'Certificate' to be prepared by the Bank and sent to the Court for being used as evidence in support of the complaint. The following is a sample of such a Form:

26 The nine-digit bank code on the cheque will enable the Court's registry to retrieve the bank's *e*-mail address, or it can be sent to their central office.

(On the letterhead / official stationery of the Bank)

.......200 ...

Certificate in terms of Rule ... of ... ... Rules

Certified that between ......200 ... (if the account is more than one year old, it is sufficient to state the beginning of the year) and ......200 ..., we were maintaining Account No. ... . of name of the account holder and title of the account and the address as recorded with the bank which was operated under the signatures of names .

Cheque No. ... . for Rs. ... ... was received in clearing on ......200 ... and was dishonoured for the reason the bank may reverify and state here the reason.

A copy of the statement of account from ......200 to ......200 is enclosed herewith. Photocopies of correspondence (if any was exchanged) with the customer (total of .... sheets) are also enclosed. Should the Hon'ble Court require any other information, we would be glad to furnish the same.

This Certificate is issued under Rule ... of ... ... Rules. The above information is certified as true and is submitted by us as a Bank directly to the Court of the Magistrate in case No. ....

Sd/- Accountant Sd/- Manager

Note: This Certificate is to be signed by an official/s who are authorised to sign a Pay Order (Manager's Cheque) for the amount of the cheque in question.

Note: With e-mail, digital signatures can be used.

74 A Certificate by the Bank on these lines will constitute sufficient material to process and adjudicate the case. It is only in case of a doubt or for some other reason that the Court may seek verification of the Certificate or call for other evidence from the Bank. The Certificate may be taken as self-proving or even constitute sufficient evidence. A new statute to replace the Banker's Books Evidence Act is also necessary.

75 The Court may also summon a copy of the personal particulars and account opening (specimen) signatures from the bank. The banks now store all these at their branch and also at the central office in electronic form and it will take less than a minute for them (on receiving a request from the court) to retrieve it and forward to the Court electronically. This would include a photograph of the account holder (accused).[27] Other information, as the facts of the case may require, can also be sent for.

Rejoinder Affidavit

76 With a Certificate from the Bank and a response from the accused, the complainant may be given an opportunity for filing a further affidavit (a

27 The recent 'Know your Customer' guidelines issued by the Reserve Bank of India have improved the situation on this score.

kind of rejoinder) in answer to the response.[28] It will reaffirm the contents of the original complaint. This affidavit can also operate as the evidence of the complainant, wherefore he may state those facts which he otherwise would have stated in his examination-in-chief at the trial. In this, he must answer the defence as also the interrogatories which the accused may have raised in his response.[29] If he does not answer, the Court may, if the question/s were relevant, raise an adverse inference, and dismiss the complaint.

77 The importance of the rejoinder affidavit lies in the fact that 'evidence' of the offence, ordinarily, lies in documents. There is also the presumption that arises, which the accused must rebut. Accordingly, the grounds and facts in that regard are best received in the 'response' argued for earlier. Depending upon the response, the complainant's stance in this rejoinder-cum-evidence affidavit will demonstrate whether an offence is made out.

78 The rejoinder affidavit having been filed, the matter will then proceed to the next stage. Section 202(1) Cr.P.C. empowers the Magistrate to require any fact/s to be investigated by the police, and for that purpose, postpone the issue of the process. Here, however, to prevent misuse of procedures – by both the complainant and the accused – it is necessary that such power is also available to the Magistrate after the issue of the process so that an attempt by any party to mislead the Court does not succeed.

Charge

79 Being a Summary trial under Chapter XXI of the Code,[30] it would (per Section 262) be tried as a summons-case. No formal charge is to be framed, but the substance of the accusations is to be stated (Section 251). This is followed by receiving the complainant's (prosecution) evidence, and then proceeding to hear the accused and taking all of such evidence as he may produce. See Section 254(1) Cr.P.C.

80 Theoretically, it can be done on the same day, though the usual practice is that the Court – after stating the substance of the accusations – posts it for another day, for which the complainant summons his witnesses and if the evidence is recorded, thereafter posts it for yet another day on which the accused's statement under Section 313 may be recorded. If the accused enters upon a defence, he may summon his witnesses or give his evidence, for which yet another hearing is fixed.

81 In practice, however, it is not so as at most of these dates, it is the accused who tries to delay the matter or there is haggling over part

---

28 This would also require pre-set specimen forms along with instruction notes so that the affidavit which is filed is proper.

29 For those cases where the accused has a genuine defence, the raising of interrogatory/ies will help expose the hollowness of many a false complaint. It, however, is not necessary to require a specific order for the purpose as the right approach would be that an accused raising unnecessary interrogatories or a complainant refusing to answer the necessary interrogatories do so at their own peril.

30 as provided for by the since inserted Section 143 in the Negotiable Instruments Act

payment and adjournment thereagainst, which process repeats itself over several hearings. The complainant too could be lackadaisical.

82 Given procedures as herein envisaged, the ideal form would be that at this or the first hearing, the Court frames the formal charges – as also the 'questions' which arise on a reading of the complaint, response and documents. Further, at this hearing, any interim orders can also be passed. This would include the power to pass a decree for recovery on consent. Rules have to be put in place, providing for a system of sending the Decree (or an interim Order for recovery of money) to the civil court for execution, where the execution procedures on the lines discussed in Chapter 7-08 supra can take over. The power to appoint a Receiver to take over possession of any asset, which is covered by the cheque, is also required.

Complainant's evidence, if any

83 With procedures like this, the bulk of the complaints would be settled by this (the Charge) stage itself, and the 'trial' in the traditional sense will be necessary only for a few cases. This is so because with pre-trial procedures as aforesaid, there will be few cases that will require oral evidence at the trial.

84 As far as the complainant's evidence (in response to the defence, if any) is concerned, the same would have been filed on an affidavit usually before framing the (informal) charge per Section 251. See para 79 supra. The accused's affidavit in reply, filed earlier, will be treated as both defence and evidence. It will, however, always be open to the Court to call for or permit any additional evidence, in which event the Court will post it for trial, i.e., for receiving the evidence of the complainant and the accused.

85 In other words, with a complaint in a comprehensive Form, opportunity for a response, the bank certificate and now an additional affidavit of the complainant wherein he meets / answers the various pleas which the accused might have raised (i.e. the rejoinder), there will be little that the complainant will need to further prove (give evidence), except maybe tender himself for cross-examination. In other words, the former would constitute sufficient material on the basis of which the Court can adjudicate upon the matter.

86 Although the right to cross-examine has to be afforded to the accused, being a special procedure, it ought to be controllable by the Court so as to prevent its misuse. Here, the nature of the defence disclosed in the affidavit (see para 63 supra) ought to be the basis.

313 Statement

87 Despite the opportunity to answer in writing / respond to the complaint as envisaged earlier, the procedural formality of Section 313 may need to be gone through. However, with the dishonoured cheque itself raising a presumption, and the material as aforesaid already on record, the Rules can dispense with it and instead leave it to the accused to adduce whatever evidence he wishes to. The '313' opportunity will be implicit.

In cases of this type, there is no need for the Court to pose the questions and the Rules can provide that the Court may as a routine dispense with his examination under clause (b) of Section 313(1).

Accused's Evidence

88 Next comes the question of the accused (the drawer of the cheque) presenting the evidence in defence. Unlike as in other criminal prosecutions, here, the accused must be expected to adduce evidence which rebuts the various presumptions raised by the dishonoured cheque.[31]

89 With Rules and Procedures as proposed here, the 'defence' of the accused will be entered into within 14 days of the service of summons, i.e., come by way of the initial response. The presumption arising from the cheque creates a 'reverse onus'. The shifting thereof to and fro will be determined by the facts and particulars as stated in the complaint and response, and the documents appended thereto. It will be only in few cases that any further or oral evidence as such would be necessary.

90 Unlike the accused at the traditional sessions trial who could neither 'see' nor 'hear' the prosecution evidence till its close, the drawer of the cheque here can see the photocopy (or the original) of the cheque as also the memo of dishonour and return. Further, the fact that the cheque was issued by him (or not) and not paid are facts within his special knowledge from day one, and it does not need any further prosecution evidence before he can be expected to respond and say what he has to.

91 Apart from the cheque, dishonour memo and notice, there must be averments in the complaint which ought to: (1) specify the consideration; and (2) state that it is still subsisting – duly supported by the affidavit. And, the opportunity to 'respond' given as aforesaid plus opportunity for a rejoinder would have helped pinpoint the controversy. True, it may be only in few cases – at best 5-10% – but if the defence (as put forward) discloses absent or failed consideration, or other facts sufficient to rebut the presumptions that arise, or any mischief by the complainant, then evidence on behalf of the accused has to be received with patience.

92 In some cases, the signatures may be disputed.[32] Other questions such as in whose handwriting the body of the cheque, including the amount and the date, has been filled, may be relevant. However, all this ought to be permitted only if sufficient facts are disclosed in the defence as initially put forward. It must be remembered that unlike other criminal (or complaint) cases, the 'presumption' arises not at the conclusion of the complainant's evidence, but at the initial stage itself – by merely placing the dishonoured instrument before the Court.

Arguments & Judgment

93 After receiving any other defence evidence, the matter can proceed to the

31 By reason of Section 262, the procedure specified for the trial of a summons case shall, ordinarily, be valid also for a summary case.

32 It may be noted that not every case of disputed signatures needs the evidence of handwriting experts. This too depends on the facts disclosed.

hearing of arguments followed by judgment. Drawing an accurate List of Events and even examining the consideration and its passing (and its subsistence), presence of other securities, etc., may be necessary. The presumptions arising from the instrument, as also onus and its shifting, rebuttal etc., can be clarified in an instruction manual (guidelines) published by the CCRI[33] as that will make the task simpler in every way.

94 Once there has been a judgment convicting the accused, alongside, an Order (more of a Decree for recovery of money) capable of execution by the civil court should also be passed. This may also include orders to proceed against any property that was covered by the amount of the cheque. Being an offence, sentencing follows, but as noted earlier, here the purpose of the complainant is more to recover his money, wherefore at times it may be more practical to defer the sentencing. However, if payment is not forthcoming, a sentence has to be ordered and served.

95 The original cheque/s, if not already filed, must be received on the court file at this stage whereupon an endorsement by way of a rubber stamp affixed like on an Exhibit be made on the face of the cheque to say:

DISCHARGED Orders on this cheque passed on ... . 200...

Court and case details. Sd/-

This will prevent avoidable confusion or later misuse of the cheque. If, however, the complainant is merely relegated to the civil court, then no such endorsement would be made, and the cheque returned.

96 These were a few thoughts and on these lines, detailed procedures for a Section 138 complaint can be developed. So done, a complaint could be disposed of in three 'hearings', or at the most five, and each hearing would not consume much of court time either. And it is only then that the purpose would stand served in real terms. So much for the procedures, though there is further detailing of procedures with reference to 'computerisation'. Some other related issues so as to make these procedures both effective as also user friendly are now stated.

7. This field of law and Computerisation

97 The advent of computerisation and information technology has changed the way in which we conduct ourselves today as compared to the way we did in the past. Likewise, banking operations have found a new form. See Chapter 8 supra. While computerisation of courts is detailed in Chapter 13 infra, some useful points on how it could be used to speed up the process of Section 138 complaints may now be noted.

98 The complaint (paras 45-52 supra) can be *e*-filed. However, a hard copy carrying the signatures on each page and an affidavit will have to be filed alongside. The cheques can be scanned and filed as a JPEG file, though (alongside) an electronic form for keying-in the particulars of the

33 Central Court Research Institute. See Topic 12 of Chapter 13 infra.

cheque including the endorsements etc. is advisable. The former is only an image file and it will be convenient to have the data in text form (and in 'fields' or 'boxes' against each column) so that it can be picked up for the purposes of the court's process–summons, orders, evidence, judgment, etc.

99 The specimen form in para 45 [at pp95 supra of this excerpt] can be developed as an electronic form, with fixed column and field numbers and also instruction notes, which appear as balloons against each column. This will increase clarity and consistency in filing, and being a standard fixed form, it will facilitate quicker uptake by the Magistrate.

100 Then, not only the summons (para 57), but also most of the Orders which are passed by the Magistrate in these cases are similar in form. A set of ten pre-formatted sample orders, which, by a click of two keys,[34] would appear on the screen (as draft specimens) would cover most of the Orders required to be passed. The case particulars will be automatically lifted by the computer and inserted in the electronic file. This can then be edited and finalised by the Magistrate and after taking a printout, signed and placed on the record. It will ensure accuracy and consistency. Even the date setting process can be computer controlled. See Topic 8 of Chapter 12 –Computers for Court Calendar (Diary) management.

101 The Order framing the charge can also be computer generated. The necessary details can appear on the screen (lifted from the complaint and the response) and inserted in the draft (specimen) 'Order', which the Magistrate can 'edit'–keep what is required, delete what is not and alter where it is necessary. A comprehensive Order framing the Charge/s (along with other pointed questions) can be turned out in a few minutes.

102 There can be sample questions, or points, which will help frame the charges. The prefatory note to the charge can also be in the form of a sample with the details of the parties and cheque being automatically lifted and inserted. Of course, the Magistrate will have to apply his mind, but the availability of a pre-keyed-in sample text on the screen will make his task much simpler and speedier.

103 Even for the evidence to be received, a structural guide could be prepared and made available to the Magistrate. It will list the points and the sequence in which the evidence would be received. With the complainant's evidence as also the defence evidence being recorded on a word processor, the facility of search, correlation and copy-paste will be available. This will, later on, help in writing out the judgment.

104 Inasmuch as the task of the Court is to do justice, questions to be (also) asked from the complainant as also from the accused can be made available to the Magistrate on the computer screen as pre-formatted text where he has to only vary/adapt them to the facts of the case and seek answers so that his conclusion best approximates with the truth.

---

34 See the discussion on pre-formatted text, macros and style sheets in Chapter 13.

105 Finally, for the judgment too, there can be a pre-set format with its headings, sub-headings and specimen matter (with checklists) under each sub-heading, which can be used by the Magistrate (by copy-paste) to turn out a final judgment in short time. Inasmuch as the claim and the defence would be there in hard copy as also soft copy, the relevant portions can be directly lifted / copied from the electronic file and pasted at the relevant places in the draft specimen of the judgment.

106 It may, however, be noted that computers, as also Case and litigation Management, will not by themselves do everything; procedural rules (with their constant updating) are also required. The former will only aid and speed up the process.

8. More thoughts towards reform in law

107 Proceeding further, first, some aspects of substantive law may be addressed. There is error in the statute's approach as to what precise act or event constitutes the offence. A reading of the statute gives an impression that (consequent to the notice under Section 138) it is the expiry of 15 days without payment, which constitutes the offence. In other words, it is the failure to pay the amount of the cheque within the stipulated time, after service of the notice, that is the offence.

108 In *D. Vinod Shivappa vs Nanda Belliappa*,[35] the Supreme Court observed:

> 9 The drawer of the cheque makes himself liable for prosecution under Section 138 of the Act if he fails to make the payment within fifteen days of the receipt of the notice given by the drawee. His failure to make the payment within the stipulated period gives rise to a cause of action to the complainant to prosecute the drawer under Section 138 of the Act.
>
> 13 … The law treats such lapses induced by inadvertence or negligence to be pardonable, provided the drawer after notice makes amends and pays the amount within the prescribed period. …

This, however, is an interpretation of the existing statute.

109 The emphasis, instead, should be on the issue and delivery of a worthless cheque and its dishonour, which offence 'compounds' itself by reason of payment within 15 days of the notice under clause (b) of the proviso. In other words, if such cheque is paid for, along with the statutory additions as herein proposed, the offence automatically compounds itself. If it is not paid, then it is the original act of the issue of the worthless cheque and its dishonour – in contradistinction to mere failure to pay consequent to such notice – which ought to be defined as an offence.[36]

110 A person commits the offence if he delivers a cheque on any bank for the

35 2006-6 SCC 456,'61,'62 = AIR 2006 SC 2179

36 Whether the offence occurred earlier and stood compounded, or, by reason of non-payment after notice, the earlier act (of issue and delivery of cheque) is by law deemed to be an offence, makes little difference in the end result, but the offence has to be, and be only, of the point of time when the cheque was delivered.

payment of money in exchange for a present consideration knowing that if it is presented within 30 days of delivery it will not be honoured by the drawee bank.[37] Hence, the statute can presume – or simply deem – fraudulent intent if payment is refused by the drawee for lack of funds upon presentation within 30 days after delivery and the accused has not tendered the holder thereof the amount due thereon, together with a service charge, within fifteen days after receiving written notice that payment was refused upon such instrument.

111 Put differently, the offence is not the failure – or the inability – to pay the cheque after notice, but delivering an instrument with the present intent to defraud. The gravamen of the offence ought to be defined by the statute as the 'fraudulent intent' with which the instrument is delivered as distinct from subsequent dishonour of a cheque not meant for immediate payment. This will also help exclude post-dated cheques.

112 As noted in paras 14 and 21 supra, the substantive law (Section 138 and allied sections) calls for a reading that excludes post-dated cheques. Even in Western countries, dishonour of a post-dated cheque is – absent special circumstances – not a criminal offence. See also the discussion in Topic 8 of Chapter 8 [excerpt at pp120 infra]. That discussion is re-emphasised here. Law must be correctly interpreted so as to exclude post-dated cheques, and if not, we must amend the statute. Further – absent sufficient reasons to the contrary – the substantive law must be in consonance with Article 11 of the International Covenant on Civil and Political Rights, 1966. Even otherwise, public policy requires that post-dated cheques be clarified as being outside the ambit of criminal law.

113 However, where a cheque was only a more convenient substitute for cash, issued in payment of a current liability, and intended to be encashed the following day or so (or immediately thereafter), the procedural law needs reform, which gives it more teeth and enables quick, convenient and effective disposal as also recovery. To that end, reform in both substantive and procedural law is called for. New laws in that regard, as part of commercial/mercantile law, which cover all aspects, need to be framed.

114 Several other aspects will also need to be identified and then covered. As one instance, the property that was the 'consideration' for the cheque being issued ought to be covered by a 'dishonoured cheque holder's lien', which the Statute – taking cue from an unpaid seller's lien – must provide for. For example, a motor car purchased and paid for by a cheque that is dishonoured ought to be covered under a lien as this and recovery of its possession permissible forthwith. A Receiver to recover possession thereof should be readily appointed. However, that principle cannot, in practical terms, be extended to payment by cheque for the food served in a restaurant or the haircut at a salon.

---

37 While for the civil law purposes the cheque may not become 'stale' till three months, for fastening liability under criminal law, 30 days ought to be the outer limit, i.e., the cheque be presented within 30 days of issue/delivery.

115 How, in practical operation of laws and procedures, problems surface and then need to be attended to by amendments from time to time may also be examined. As a sample, we take the notice contemplated under proviso (clause (b)) to Section 138. This is considered an integral part of the offence, for it is only on failure to make the payment consequent to the notice that the complaint can be filed. In other words, unless a notice has been served and the amount remains unpaid, no complaint lies.

116 Many times, the holder (payee) of the dishonoured cheque wanting to serve the notice may not be aware of the correct address of the drawer;[38] or being aware of a wrong address, he may send a notice to that (wrong) address. Also, the notice may have been sent to the correct address, but the drawer may have (mischievously) not received it or kept evidence that he could not have received it while the returned AD card bears some scribble. After the complaint is filed and summons issued, objections on these count/s are raised, and consume unnecessary amount of court time.

117 Now, as a solution to this problem, the procedural law can provide for the following:

1 The bank on which the dishonoured cheque was drawn would provide the address of the drawer (their customer) as recorded with them, upon a request in writing by the payee, enclosing therewith a photocopy of the cheque (attested by the payee's bankers) and return memo, and a fee of Rs. 200.

2 Whenever an objection as to the service of the notice or its validity is raised, the Court, unless it feels that the complainant was lacking in bona fides, may order that the proceedings at the hearing operate as the notice, and adjourn the matter by 15 days so that if payment is made on or before the next hearing, the complaint can be consigned to the record room,[39] otherwise the objection would stand rejected and the complaint can proceed.

This was one sample to demonstrate how the very many problems that arise in practice can be remedied by updating the statute/rules and thus prevent waste of court time and delays.

118 Then, being a complaint case, the complainant has to be personally present at every hearing, which is unnecessary for this type of cases. Appearance through a specified attorney or even an advocate should be permissible. The accused may however have to appear unless he is granted exemption. In any case, if the postings/hearings are going to be no more than a few, this would cease to be a problem.

119 Often, where the payee is a corporation or other juristic entity, the problem of proving the 'authority' to lodge a complaint arises. Here too, the Rules need to provide a Form for the authority/attorney as also for

---

38 which address the drawer's bank generally refuses to disclose

39 See similar discussion on notices and objections in paras 23 to 26 of Topic 4 of Chapter 7-03 at pp1039 supra.

the affidavit. The Rules also need to provide for raising the appropriate presumptions so that these documents can be sufficiently proved by way of another affidavit. Para 71 earlier had referred to banker's certificates, which (this time from the payee's bankers) can be used to advantage.

120 Appending a Certificate by a Banker – to the effect that they have been maintaining an account for the payee of the cheque and that for withdrawal from the account the signature of the person[40] attested by them suffices – will help remove doubts. The complaint by such person can, based on such certificate, be treated as validly instituted by the juristic entity. It is only in an extremely rare case that the Court would need to go further into this question.

121 The use of cheques as security causes problems, one aspect of which is complaints against the directors of an ailing finance company, for it is physically impossible for them to appear in all the courts all over the country all the time. Some method will have to be worked out for the clubbing of complaints against drawers, or at least adjusting the court dates / appearance. With cheques being issued in large numbers – and often post-dated – and sent all over the country, this becomes all the more necessary.

122 The facts in *Narinderjit Singh Sahni vs Union of India*[41] bring out the nature of the problem. Here, the Supreme Court felt that with accused facing Section 138 cases all over India, the Central Government should evolve certain formula or procedure, so that the accused will not complain of undue harassment while the complainants can also have the benefit of early conclusion of the trial. A similar issue again came up before the Supreme Court in *Pramod Kumar Saxena vs Union of India*[42] where an ex-Director of a company, facing 48 cases in six different States and having remained in jail for more than 10 years, was granted some relief. The recent judgment in *Harman Electronics vs National Panasonic*[43] adopts a practical approach in the matter and will help prevent abuse by complainants. The problem, nevertheless, calls for a reform in the statute.

123 A provision for passing an Order (decree) for recovery – whether on consent or on judicial adjudication, and at any stage of the proceedings – must be there. Rules or a system of sending the Decree (or an interim Order) for recovery of money to the civil court for execution will also have to be put in place where execution procedures on the lines discussed in Chapter 7-08 supra can then take charge.

124 On conclusion of the proceedings, the Court, along with an Order for recovery of the amount of the cheque, would also pass an Order for

40 if he be the person who has filed the complaint

41 2002-2 SCC 210 = AIR 2001 SC 3810

42 2008-9 SCC 685

43 Criminal Appeal 2021/08 decided by the Supreme Court on 12.12.2008.

payment of interest at a rate which may be specified by a notification (as discussed in Topic 9 of Chapter 4 at pp259 supra) with half-yearly rests from the date appearing on the cheque till the date of payment. The interest awarded by the Court should carry a 3-4% surcharge – for a dishonoured cheque as distinct from a commercial or any other debt – i.e., if the statutory rate is 11%, the Order here should be for 14-15%.

125 Payment after a Notice consequent to dishonour (under Section 138 and which requires payment of the amount) should also attract a 'charge' (at a prescribed scale) to operate as a deterrent. A 'notice fee' of Rs. 550 plus certain percentage[44] of the cheque amount (as the Rules may specify) should be treated as a statutory addition to the cheque amount, payable by the drawer to the payee. Interest from the date of dishonour to the date of issue of the Banker's cheque (Pay order) at the statutory rate (but without any surcharge as stated in the para above) be also included.

126 There are also times when a complaint and the defence put forward raises complicated questions in which event neither is it proper to dismiss nor is it proper to proceed to a criminal trial. In such situations, the Rules can make a provision for paying some money or furnishing security and sending the matter to the civil court for trial. A provision for 'no fault, no admission and without prejudice payment'[45] to the complainant pending trial may also be put in place. This would not (technically speaking) compound the offence and the complaint can be revived after the decision of the civil court.

127 This will also be helpful because there are many cases where the defence is bona fide in the sense that the complainant is in the wrong and ultimately because of error in the final judgment (which is based on the evidence adduced), a distortion could result. A provision as this would encourage payment and, ultimately, even if the accused is held guilty, such payments could be considered as mitigating the crime, if not absolving the accused. He will, in any case, have to also pay costs of both proceedings. At the same time, if it is found that the complaint was false, the complainant would have to bear the brunt for having committed an offence against the administration of justice. Doing so will deter speculative or non-bonafide complaints.

128 An Order directing payment of costs to the complainant (payee) must be the rule. The amount thereof be sufficient to cover his costs fully and also compensate him for the time and trouble. Costs to the Court for the time consumed are also to be reimbursed. See para 40 supra.

129 There is also need for a penalty (fine) payable to the State (as already provided for by Section 138) to act as a deterrent. The amount thereof ought to depend on the amount of the cheque, the circumstances in

---

44 Say, 5% up to Rs.20,000; 3% up to Rs. One lakh; and 1% for over Rs. One lakh.

45 This will be 'with recourse', that is to say, if the complaint is dismissed, the payment would be refundable.

which it was issued and dishonoured, the conduct before the Court, and generally on the facts of each case viewed in the light of such guidelines as may be issued. If the circumstances are such, or, particularly, if the amount remains unpaid, a jail term be ordered. This will also deter dishonour of cheques in general. However, doing so for post-dated cheques would not be proper.

130 At the same time, to not make a provision for instalments,[46] the need for which is both an economic and a human necessity, is only encouraging contest and perjury. To insist on a hard line approach of 'Bring money today, whatever be the source from which you procure, or go to jail', is wrong. The ground realities ought not to be ignored. See also the related discussion in Topic 4 (providing for a Cushion) of Chapter 8 supra.

131 In practice, however, the courts often – and rightly – take the approach of orally observing: 'Bring at least something' (which is a form of instalments) and on payment of that adjourn the matter to another day, on which day the process may repeat itself. While such an approach, as far as justice and fair play as also practicalities are concerned, cannot be really found fault with, it causes waste of court time in avoidable haggling.

132 What is required, therefore, is a provision for instalments (which may be fixed by the Court) and at a rate of interest which is not concessional but practically high, i.e., 3% above the notified rate.[47] The 'extra high' rate of interest for the instalment period will be applicable only for the period till full payment is made. This will act as an incentive for pre-payment. Of course, the instalments will be with a default clause, full interest, penal interest, costs, and there will still be a 'sentence' for the initial offence, though it is a different matter that upon payment being made, some leniency may be shown, or the sentence may be restricted to a fine.

133 Payments to the complainant are best made by a special instrument as envisaged in Topic 11 of Chapter 14 infra, where a sample has also been given. Further, a Form for stating, calculating and reconciling rival versions of account (payments and receipts), and adjudicating upon the principal, the interest and the payment of the instalments, will also have to be developed. The right thing would be to have a prescribed Form, ask each party to fill it up, append at the bottom a certificate-cum-verification-cum-affidavit as to the correctness and submit the same to the Court. The Court (and, if need be, with the aid of support staff) can determine the right figures by placing the two versions side by side.

134 Before our courts today, there is – by one or the other – extensive perjury

46 particularly, when it relates to post-dated cheques and assuming their dishonour is continued to be treated as a criminal offence

47 Para 124 already points out the need for a higher interest rate for defaulted cheques. The interest should be compound with quarterly rests so as to take away the incentive for non-payment or delay. See the discussion in Chapter 4. The number of instalments, however, should be sufficient.

and abuse. Complaints under Section 138 are no exception. Although some courts may not tend to think so, it is not always that a complaint by the holder of a cheque is true and bona fide. There can be, in fact are, several forms of 'abuse of process' by him or by the accused – and the Court must not ignore these. In either event, whosever is in the wrong must bear the brunt of it. This is the only way the procedures can be made efficient and serve the purpose for which they are intended.

135 The discussion in Topics 2 to 10 of Chapter 11 infra will, in this regard, be applicable. If any false averment in a complaint or affidavit, or a false document in support of a complaint, is noticed, the Court should not hesitate in taking action, which may mean a jail term for making false averments in (or attaching false document/s with) the complaint or the defence, in addition to that for the offence. Readiness and sternness on this score will prevent false complaints. If a complaint is false, the fact that it is 'compromised' with the accused should be no ground to not take action. For the system to function, purity in the presentation – of the complaint as also the response by the accused – has to be ensured.

136 There is need for a new set of statutory provisions (substantive and procedural) as also detailed Rules – at quite some variance from those at present – for processing such complaints. The right approach here would be to have a separate statute combining the substantive and procedural law relating to dishonoured cheques. It can be titled as the 'Cheques and Related Offences Code [Act ... of 200...]'. Apart from Sections 138 to 147 of the Negotiable Instruments Act, several provisions from other statutes can be incorporated in it. The substantive law would be contained in the first part while procedure will be provided by the second or a separate part of the statute.

137 The procedural part of this Code will of course give power to the Central Government as also the High Court to frame Rules, prescribe Forms and issue guidelines, or to amend them from time to time. The power of 'Forms' needs to be harnessed and there will be need to provide guidelines and instruction notes as an appendix to the Rules.[48] These guidelines, instruction notes and the specimen Forms are of great importance. The CCRI along with the Indian Banks' Association[49] can help develop the right pattern for the Forms – for the complaint, response as also other matters – which will help the Court to reach to the truth almost at the first look itself.

138 To be able to make full use, it is not just putting rules, procedures and other systems in place; it also requires informing the public. Therefore, once the Rules are in place (and hopefully, the substantive law is also amended), it will be worthwhile to make an official publication of a small

48 A simple illustration is of the two-page rules and notes at the end of a passport application form.

49 See the discussion in Chapter 8 at pp2~ and in Topic 12 of Chapter 13 infra.

guide. It can describe the substantive law on this score and also the procedures to be followed – Rules, guidelines and Forms, instruction notes, etc. – while moving a complaint, responding to a complaint and otherwise generally dealing with these issues. Permission can be granted to private publishers to republish this, with their own additional notes.

139 This publication (booklet) be available for a small price so that it is not just the lawyer, but also the trader, banker or any other, who can purchase it and then apprise himself of the law on the subject. The same booklet should also contain a fair guide to the accused, i.e., the person whose cheque was dishonoured. In fact, for a subject like this, publication of an informative booklet is essential.

140 These being some thoughts towards evolving and putting in place special procedures for complaints relating to dishonoured cheques, let us then see how to go about it. It will need preparing a draft for the Code, which will contain the substantive as also procedural law. Here too, for the procedural part, as also the Rules and Forms, a wide power to amend will have to be left with the Central Government or the High Court – so as to not require a Parliamentary legislation to do the needful.

141 Laying down a fine set of procedures and forms tailored to the subject will not be the end. With feedback from the judicial Magistrates who decide such cases (as contemplated in Topic 13 of Chapter 13 infra) and from others who can contribute to fine-tuning the laws, we can develop the right set of substantive and procedural laws on this score.

142 Chapter 12 infra discusses Case and litigation Management. Section 138 complaints, instead of being distributed over all Magistrates (depending upon the Police District where the cheque was dishonoured or the accused resides), be made triable at the Magistrate's Court which covers the District's commercial centre. Further, the feasibility of having separate special courts exercising a tailored combination of civil and criminal jurisdiction to deal with claims / complaints based on dishonoured cheques should also be considered. Furthermore, a person who has had a few years' experience as a bank clerk ought to be posted as an assistant to the Magistrate hearing these matters.

143 This is another field of law and procedure in which a Magistrate (who is able to operate a computer) can have standard (pre-set) Forms and upon receiving a complaint, (his support staff) can key-in the data therefrom, issue summons and carry out further proceedings in, or process, the case with lightening speed. If there is a field where the courts can follow something on the lines of a conveyor belt mass production technique and yet not let a false complaint pass through, it is this one.

144 Topic 9 of Chapter 12 speaks of a pilot project. When it comes to trying Section 138 complaints, a pilot project would serve the purpose – of modernising criminal courts, introducing computerisation, and convincing

all concerned of its benefits. With 38 lakh complaint cases under Section 138 pending in courts all over the country, the Law Commission, in its 213rd Report on "Fast Track Magisterial Courts for Dishonoured Cheque Cases" (Nov / Dec 2008), has recommended the setting up of fast-track courts to decide such cases. Possibly, we can consider implementing the procedural reform proposed herein with the new set-up.

9. The resultant effect on cheques and dishonour

145 With revised Rules and an efficient justice system, fewer cases of dishonour of cheques will occur, but whatever be the number, the systems are bound to be far more effective than they are today. Of the few who still allow their cheques to be dishonoured, hopefully, most would concede to an Order (decree) for recovery at the first hearing itself, whereafter matters can be disposed of by a levy of costs payable both to the complainant and the Court as also an appropriate fine to be paid to the State. For others, the Certificate from the bank can (usually) be treated as sufficient, and after recording the evidence of the complainant and giving an opportunity to the defence, the matter can proceed to judgment followed by sentencing.

146 With rules and procedures like this, not only would the time consumption for processing and trial of a complaint be drastically reduced, but given adequate support staff, the productivity of a typical Magistrate will also be much more than that at present. The result would be that even with the existing number of Magistrates, other than the required processing and trial time, we may be able to have no 'waiting time'. Once the waiting time is minimised, more than anything else, the number of dishonoured cheques and, thus, accrual of litigation, will be drastically reduced, for now the message shall go out that the penalty will be swift and effective. Simply, it will achieve credibility in transacting business through cheques.

147 If the clearing of cheques by the banks has turned electronic and almost instantaneous, there is no reason why procedures for complaints of dishonoured cheques should not attempt to do or be likewise. So done, the criminal procedures will be able to adapt themselves to deal with dishonoured cheques in the electronic age – as compared to a murder trial before a jury – and serve the needs of the day in true earnest. Apart from doing justice to the holder of a dishonoured cheque, this could pave the way for computerisation of courts, for people will begin to see the benefits.

Rest of sub topic 3 of Topic 14 has not been excerpted.

☆ ☆ ☆

Excerpt from Topic 8 of Chapter 8

3. Prohibit use of Cheques as security to cover Debts

1 A 'Cheque' – which most of us use to make or receive payments – is a Bill of Exchange drawn on a Banker. It is an order on a bank purporting to be drawn upon a deposit of funds for the payment of a specified sum of money, on presentation, to the person named in the document, or to another on his order, or to the bearer. It bears a date and is payable (by the bank upon which it is drawn) on demand. It can also be made 'account payee'. In other words, a cheque is a contractual promise by the maker of the instrument (person signing the cheque) that it may be presented at the maker's (drawer's) bank for cash on demand or for a transfer of credit to the payee's account through inter-bank clearing. These definitions for a cheque coined in the 19th century still hold good.

2 Cheques are extensively used as a mode or medium of making payment for goods or services. They offer several advantages:

- i the need to carry cash (with its attendant dangers and risks) is obviated;
- ii problems of counting errors and fake notes are avoided;
- iii they can be sent by post;
- iv there arises a certain record of payment – debit in the drawer's account with corresponding credit in the payee's – which also helps in the maintaining of accounts; and
- v a completed cheque transaction is difficult to dispute, nor can it be (very exceptional cases apart) altered or manipulated.

Although the Credit Card (or the Debit/Charge Card) is gaining ground, a cheque – particularly for large amounts – will always retain its position.

3 To give more credence to a cheque that is issued, the Negotiable Instruments Act was amended in the year 1988 to insert Sections 138 to 142,[50] and again in the year 2002 to insert Sections 143 to 147. This enabled the holder (the payee), in case of dishonour of the cheque, to approach the criminal court for punishment of the drawer as a means of enforcing the amount covered by the cheque. The practical operation of criminal law and procedures in relation to Section 138 for dishonoured cheques is discussed in Topic 14 (sub-topic 3) of Chapter 10 infra. The discussion there pleads a case for reform in criminal procedures to make them more efficient and effective, while the discussion here seeks to exclude post-dated cheques from the ambit of criminal law; in fact, puts forward a case for prohibiting the use of post-dated cheques as security.

4 Prior to the 1988 amendment, in *Rachana Flour Mills vs Lal Chand Bhanagadiya*,[51] while rejecting an argument that dishonour of a post-dated cheque was a criminal offence, it was held:

---

50 inserted by Section 4 of Act 66 of 1988 (w.e.f. 1.04.1989)

51 [1987] 62 Company Cases 15 = 1985-2 Andhra Law Times 508

24 On the above conspectus, the principles that emerge are:

(1) Reading in combination Sections 6, 30, 31, and 91 to 94 of the Negotiable Instruments Act, a drawer of a cheque cannot be held criminally liable on the cheque being dishonored unless it is established that he knew at the time of drawing the cheque there was no money in the bank and that he intended to cheat the payee.

(2) A post-dated cheque in payment of goods already received is mere promise to pay on a future date and a broken promise is not a criminal offence, ...

Consequent to the amendment of the statute, the position has changed.

5 When a post-dated cheque is written or drawn, it is only a bill of exchange, and with the passage of time, on the date which is written thereon, it becomes a 'cheque' within the meaning of the Negotiable Instruments Act so as to attract the provision of Section 138 thereof. The post-dated cheque, non-payment of which became punishable as an offence – delays in the criminal courts apart – suddenly appeared to banks and financiers as a very convenient mode of securing their debts.

6 Today, if a borrower were to go to the bank for a loan of, say, ten lakhs of rupees, which he would repay over five years with interest at the rate of, say, 12% per annum (with half-yearly rests), the bank would promptly calculate the EMI (equated monthly instalment)–which, for this amount, period and rate of interest, would be (22,244.45) – ask the borrower to open a separate account; receive 60 signed post-dated cheques (dated first of every calendar month for the next five years) for Rs. 22,244.45 each; and only then release the money.

7 Now, if the borrower were unable to repay the loan, a complaint under Section 138 would be filed against him where the fear of jail term would work as the 'mode of', or the force behind, recovery.

8 At times, the practice adopted is of receiving two signed blank cheques (usually halfway down the series). These are retained by the creditor and when about 30 cheques have been encashed, the debtor is sent for and is required to sign a fresh set of post-dated cheques in replacement of the still-to-be encashed cheques, including the two blank cheques. The plain threat is:

> You confirm the debit balance, and that all transactions of the past and the account are correct, and give us these new post-dated cheques. Otherwise, we will fill up the blank cheques issued earlier by you for an amount, which we want, and then file a Section 138 complaint.

What option does a debtor have but to relent? He has little help at law.

9 The discussion here should not be understood as meaning that a debtor can avoid paying back the loan or his dues. Every measure that can enforce recovery should be put in place by law and systems–except that to

send him to jail for mere inability to pay a future debt is simply not fair. It is no different than sending goons to kidnap him till his family pays up.

10 Let us examine the problem further. There are two parts: (1) delivery of a post-dated cheque as forming the basis for a criminal offence; and (2) issue of cheques as security for a loan or any other credit. In *Babu Xavier vs Lal Chand Munoth*,[52] the Court analysed the provisions of Sections 138 and 139 as applicable to a post-dated cheque that was dishonoured. This judgment was overruled by the Supreme Court in *Anil Kumar Sawhney vs Gulshan Rai*.[53]

11 In *Shri Ishar Alloy Steels Ltd vs Jayaswals Neco Ltd*,[54] the Supreme Court observed:

> 7 When a post-dated cheque is written or drawn, it is only a Bill of exchange. The post-dated cheque become a cheque under the Act on the date which is written on the said cheque and the six months' period has to be reckoned, for the purposes of Section 138 of the Act, from the said date.

The view was reiterated in *Ashok Yeshwant Badave vs Surendra Madhavrao Nighojakar*,[55] where they said:

> 19 Under Section 6 of the Negotiable Instruments Act a 'Cheque' is also a bill of exchange but it is drawn on a banker and payable on demand. A Bill of exchange even though drawn on a banker, if it is not payable on demand, is not a cheque. A 'post-dated cheque' is not payable till the date that is shown thereon arrives and will become cheque on the said date and prior to that date the same remains bill of exchange.

It is submitted that for Section 138 proceedings, this view requires reconsideration.

12 The problem further arises when the cheque dishonoured is issued as a security cheque. Law is not clear whether such cheque can be submitted to the consequences of Section 138 of the Act or not. Section 139 reads:

> It shall be presumed, unless the contrary is proved, that the holder of a cheque received the cheque of the nature referred to in Section 138 for the discharge, in whole or in part, of any debt or other liability.

This shows that at the time the cheque is received (delivered), the liability must pre-exist, and if the delivery of the cheque is prior in point of time to the grant of loan – as it usually is, for unless the post-dated cheques are first received, the creditor does not advance the loan – the presumption cannot apply. Another contention raised is that the words

52 [1992] 74 Company Cases 716 (Madras) = 1990 TLNJ (Crl) 121

53 1993-4 SCC 424,'30 = 1993-6 JT 280= [1994] 79 Company Cases 150 (SC). See also the observations in *Goaplast (P) Ltd. vs Chico Ursula D'Souza* 2003-3 SCC 232 = AIR 2003 SC 2035.

54 2001-3 SCC 609 = AIR 2001 SC 1161

55 2001-3 SCC 726 = AIR 2001 SC 1315

'the date on which it is drawn' in the proviso to Section 138 refer to the date on which it is written out, and that (as distinct from the future date that it may bear) is the relevant one, wherefore a post-dated cheque would stand excluded.

13 On this issue (use of post-dated cheques as security for loans), in *Dr. Sampathkumar vs Ms. Dr. K.G.V. Lakshmi, GCIM, Lakshmi Health Centre*,[56] the Karnataka High Court held:

> A cheque whether issued for repayment of a loan or as a security makes little difference under Section 138 of the Act. In the event of a dishonour, legal consequences are same without distinction.

But there is no reasoning in support of that conclusion. An observation (perhaps one in passing) of the Supreme Court in *M.S. Narayana Menon vs State of Kerala*[57] may also be cited here:

> 52 ... If the defence is accepted as probable the cheque therefor cannot be held to have been issued in discharge of the debt as, for example, if a cheque is issued for security or for any other purpose the same would not come within the purview of Section 138 of the Act.

True, there is no finding as such, but it is submitted that with respect to the dishonour of security cheques, the position is not as clear as many contend it to be. In any case, this was about the existing statute and the judicial opinion, and as this work is directed towards reform, we may proceed to address the right or the wrong of it on principle.

14 A cheque bearing a date that is subsequent to the date on which the cheque was drawn and delivered is called a post-dated cheque. A cheque has been defined as 'a draft drawn on a bank and payable on demand'. A post-dated cheque, since it is not payable on demand, cannot satisfy the true definition of a cheque. The post-dating of the cheque creates an extension of credit, even if it be only for a week, and changes the situation.

15 Section 46 of the Negotiable Instruments Act, 1881 provides:

> The making, acceptance or indorsement of a promissory note, bill of exchange or cheque is completed by delivery, actual or constructive.

That being so, or everything being complete upon delivery, it is difficult to understand how something not relating to an act of that time can, some months or years later, be termed an offence. It is basic that any offence in this regard has to carry both *mens rea* and proof of some act at the time of delivery.

16 In *Commissioner of Income-Tax vs Ogale Glass Works*,[58] the Supreme Court, while considering what would be the date of payment for a cheque –date of delivery or date of encashment–took the view that:

---

56 2006 Criminal Law Journal 2267 = [2006] 132 Company Cases 160 = 2006-4 Banking Cases 209 = 2006-3 Karnataka Law Journal 333

57 2006-6 SCC 39 = AIR 2006 SC 3366

58 AIR 1954 SC 429 = 1955-1 SCR 185 = [1954] 25 ITR 529

> 11 ... the cheques not having been dishonoured but having been cashed, the payment related back to the dates of the receipt of the cheques and in law the dates of payments *were the dates of the delivery of the cheques.* (emphasis supplied)

If the 'date of delivery' be all-important (and which it ought to be), the question of an offence being committed at a later date is ruled out.

17 A post-dated cheque implies on its face a present insufficiency of funds and represents a promise to discharge a present obligation on a future date. Absent fraudulent intent, the transaction essentially becomes one of extending credit to the drawer. A post-dated cheque is in effect a promissory note – the very act of dating the cheque ahead being tantamount to an express declaration that it would not be paid if presented at once.

18 Criminal law, or Section 138 proceedings, ought to be confined to only those cases where a person receives goods or services, and instead of paying for them (simultaneously) in cash, chooses to pay by cheque, which cheque is not honoured. In such cases (where he fails to pay even after notice), he should be punished with a jail term. The use of post-dated cheques as collateral security for loans is wrong. A cheque should be confined to being an instrument for making payment.

19 Even if a person (drawer) received goods or services sometime in the past and made a payment on his debt with a cheque that bounced, it ought not to be a crime punishable with jail because the payee did not 'lose out' on anything or surrender anything by relying on a representation of the worth of the cheque. Essentially, the drawer owed a payment and just still has not made it, and can be sued in a civil court as if the payee has received no payment at all – with the cheque being added evidence in support of his claim.

20 So much so that if the drawer asks the payee to hold the cheque for a few days before depositing it, and the payee agrees, the case is no longer a criminal matter. This amounts to the drawer saying:

> This cheque is not as good as cash today. I plan to make it good, and you will be paid for your merchandise/services in the future.

Truly speaking, then, it is a debt to be recovered as a civil case. The same applies if the drawer gives and the payee accepts a post-dated cheque. The legal significance of post-dating is that the cheque is not expected to be good until the date on the cheque arrives. If such a cheque bounces, it is equivalent to – and no more than – the drawer not honouring a Promissory Note or a Guarantee Bond.

21 To reiterate, a post-dated cheque, which is in effect but a representation on the part of the payer/drawer that on a future date he will have funds with which to satisfy it, is only an obligation on his part to pay the sum involved on a future date. One may ask: what is the material difference

– as a species of commercial paper – between such a cheque and a promissory note? Can it be seriously contended that failure to pay a note by reason of financial inability is a crime? The barbarous practice of imprisoning a person for mere inability to pay a debt – the obligation not being the result of wrongdoing – is a thing of the past.

22 For the above reasons, cheques written as security in loan 'transactions' (where money is loaned in exchange for a post-dated cheque/s) ought not to be covered by the criminal law. There is essentially an understanding between the parties that the cheques are not good on the date the loan is received, and that none of them is expected to be good until the future time or the 'post-date' arrives. Such a cheque is essentially a Promissory Note, or collateral for the loan. The payee can indeed sue in a civil court to recover the loan, but filing criminal charges is not appropriate.

23 Looked at differently, if the payee or holder knows, or has good and sufficient reason to believe, that the drawer did not have sufficient funds on deposit to the drawer's credit at the time of the delivery of the cheque to the drawee to ensure payment, it is simply a case of extending credit. Further, a post-dated cheque cannot be a 'cheque' within the contemplation of a criminal worthless cheque law because such an instrument – at the time of its issue and delivery – is not payable on demand. Furthermore, the holders of these post-dated cheques almost always have other 'securities' with them.[59] The presence of security is also a pointer to the fact that post-dated cheques cannot be included within the ambit of criminal law.

24 To support a criminal action, the cheque must have been given for present consideration. The crux of the offence is similar to a theft of an item or services received through the fraudulent presentation of worthless paper when immediate payment is expected. Anything that separates in time the exchange of goods/services with money, will negate the concept of present consideration and make it a case of 'credit'. Stated simply, a present consideration cannot include a post-dated cheque.

25 Let us test the fundamentals of the proposition. We assume a cheque is issued on a particular day, say, 1.04.2006, and is dated, say, 31.03.2007 – i.e., not for immediate payment or on demand. Stopping here for a moment, one thing is clear: there can be no offence during the 12-month period ending 31.03.2007.[60] The question that then arises is: When does the offence take place:

1 On 31.03.2007 when the date arrives? or

2 On, say, 5.04.2007, when the cheque is dishonoured by the Bank?

The answer to each must be in the negative because neither can movement of time constitute an offence nor can, strictly speaking, failure to pay a past debt constitute an offence.

---

59 say, mortgage of immovable property or hypothecation of movable property, and particularly so if it was purchased on credit/instalments

60 because it is not a negotiable instrument till then

26 Further, if the drawer had died in the meantime, in the year 2006, would the offence still have taken place? These are some of the questions which need to be addressed. In any case, the discussion here argues a case for exclusion of post-dated cheques from the ambit of criminal law, if need be, by statutory amendment.

27 Let us examine further. Today, if a person has issued several hundred post-dated cheques and he has a genuine business failure, even insolvency laws have no protection for him, and as we keep hearing, he may be driven to suicide. This is certainly not the purpose of law in modern society. One may visualise with a few hundred complaints under Section 138 pending all over the country, what option does a person have?

28 Proceedings under Section 138 should be restricted only to cheques given for immediate encashment because the act of receiving goods / services with a promise of simultaneous / immediate payment is the reason for writing out the cheque. It is a breach of that which forms a cause or justification for a complaint / prosecution and not the ability / expectancy of doing so (making payment) in future. It is this (the former) which should attract criminal law – quite like giving fake currency notes would – and not mere inability to pay at a future date.

29 The International Covenant on Civil and Political Rights, 1996 clearly states that no one shall be imprisoned merely on the ground of inability to fulfil a contractual obligation. See Article 11. In other words, sending to jail for mere inability to repay the debt is prohibited. Although it (the Covenant) may not have been made part of our Municipal Law, yet we cannot avoid the principles. It is neither a statutory due nor something that became due by reason of abuse of the Court's process – as, for instance, damages, costs or fines specially ordered by a court of law.

30 In *Jolly George Varghese vs Bank of Cochin*,[61] the Supreme Court ruled:

> 10 … It is too obvious to need elaboration that to cast a person in prison because of his poverty and consequent inability to meet his contractual liability is appalling. To be poor, in this land of *Daridra Narayana*, is no crime and to recover debts by the procedure of putting one in prison is to flagrantly violative of Article 21 unless there is proof of the minimal fairness of his wilful failure to pay in spite of his sufficient means and absence of more terribly pressing claims on his means such as medical bills to treat cancer or other grave illness. Unreasonableness and unfairness in such a procedure is inferrable from Article 11 of the Covenant. …

See also the decision in *Ram Narayan Agarwal vs State of U.P.*[62] Placing a debtor in prison is not a civilised society's norm for recovery of debt.

31 Further, there is a world of difference between a cheque substituting

61 1980-2 SCC 360,'7 = AIR 1980 SC 470

62 1983-4 SCC 276 = AIR 1984 SC 1213

that which would have been a cash payment on one side and grant of credit on the other. If a payee willingly accepts a post-dated cheque in exchange for merchandise sold or a service rendered, he is only extending credit to the drawer of the cheque. The position is worse when it is operating merely as a security for a loan taken, to be repaid on a future date. Taking cheques post-dated by months or even years, and yet including them within the ambit of Section 138, is far from proper.

32 Section 138 was inserted in the year 1989. Let us examine the criminal complaints filed thereunder over the last one decade. There were thousands and thousands of complaints, and maybe even a million, based on dishonoured cheques. Let us ask ourselves the following question:

> What percentage of the total complaints related to cheques which were signed and delivered with an intention that they may be presented to the bank on the next or the following working day (for consideration whether as goods, services, etc. which had passed, but not a loan taken) and how many of them were there – post-dated (or even undated) – and issued only as 'security' for future payment?

Stated simply: Was the intent one of payment *in præsenti* or *in futuro*?

33 It will bear repetition that analysing the complaints under Section 138 that were filed over the last decade, one would get the following impression (conservative):

		Percentage
1	Cheques issued purely as a security for a debt payable in future	95
2	Cheques issued with the professed intention that they would be encashed in the next few days	3
3	Cheques (blank or otherwise) signed by the accused which the complainant got hold of either in good faith or wrongly, and the complainant misuses them	2

34 The second item (3%) can be further sub-divided into three categories:

A. dispute regarding sufficiency/failure of the consideration for the cheque such as the goods/services paid for by the cheque turning out to be improper/defective – 2%;

B. delay in or failure of expected credit in the account or some other unforeseen problem but there was every intention to pay – 0.5%;

C. handing over the cheque where the giver of the cheque had no intention to pay – 0.5%.

Out of these, sub-category A is mostly settled with some give and take, sub-category B is quickly settled (paid), but sub-category C has fewer chances of settlement and goes on being contested for quite some time.

35 The third item (2%) of false complaints arises because of theft, trickery or other forms of frauds, including coercion and undue influence, in getting the cheques signed in blank. Or, it could be misuse of a cheque given in good faith with blank signatures, or loss by the one to whom they were

given and misuse by a third person.[63] Usually, in this third category too, the complainant is able to extract something from the accused to 'settle'.

36 Thus, we have a provision in criminal law which defines future non-payment as an offence and under the threat of jail, seeks to enforce payment of a debt, and so even if a person may have lost all his worth in a cyclone, flood or earthquake. Let us take an illustration. A self-employed professional purchases a motor car on instalments, which are secured by 36 deferred payment (post-dated) cheques in addition to hypothecation of the car as also an assignment of its insurance. He expects those cheques to be honoured and paid for, not from what he owns today but from what he is going to earn each month in the ensuing three years.

37 A month later, while driving the car so purchased, a city transport bus rams into it. The car is damaged and his legs are broken. He is confined to the hospital for months. Unable to earn, and the hospital bills being his first priority, what he receives is summons from a criminal court. On account of his broken legs, he is unable to attend the Court and it is followed by NBWs. It may take long for him to recover and still longer for the insurance company to settle the claim (at what amount is a different question), but the more important question is: Was a provision like Section 138 meant for this?

38 Take another illustration, and this is of an entrepreneur borrowing money from a bank to buy machinery, and signing and handing over 60 post-dated cheques for the next five years to the bank which financed the machine. Now, by reason of change in government policy or the dumping of goods by a foreign country, the plant & machinery become useless. The industry closes down. Is it a case for insolvency or is it a case for jail term under Section 138? The 'sickness' of an industry (genuine or feigned, apart) is, under the present law, no defence to a Section 138 prosecution of the Directors who signed the cheque.[64]

39 Take yet another illustration. A multi-national company is marketing popular and expensive equipment, using which the purchasers render job services to customers for a fee. The R&D Section of the company develops a new model, which is more efficient, i.e., it gives more productivity at lesser cost. The development is kept back as a commercial secret. The company is, however, faced with a stock of a few thousand current model machines. Now, it can always sell them for a discount before introducing the new model, but that would mean only a few takers. Therefore, what it does is to float a scheme where the purchasers can pay for it[65] in interest-free instalments over a period of seven years.

---

63 Once again, these figures are only an impression.

64 See *Kusum Ingots & Alloys Ltd vs Pennar Peterson Securities Ltd* 2000-2 SCC 745 = AIR 2000 SC 95.

65 the equipment which is to be soon replaced by the newer model

40 Lured by the seemingly attractive offer, many people line up to purchase the machines. For the future instalments, the company insists upon receiving post-dated cheques. Since the period was seven years with six months' moratorium, the purchasers issue 84 post-dated cheques alongside a cheque for a very small down payment. Once stocks are cleared and the post-dated cheques are in 'stock', the new model is introduced. By introduction of the new model in the market, the old model is rendered as good as worthless. Not being able to find any business on those machines, the purchasers, and understandably, are not able to pay, i.e, honour, the post-dated cheques on presentation.

41 In such a situation, should Section 138 be applied against the purchasers? Or should the provisions of criminal law be used against the company who so conducted itself against the gullible purchasers? The questions need some pondering over. These were only a few illustrations. There can be hundreds of such illustrations.

42 A cheque, it must be remembered, is a more convenient mode of payment than delivery of cash. That is the purpose of a cheque and it is really for those cases where a person was intending to make simultaneous payment by cash, which he substituted by cheque, and that cheque was not honoured, that a provision like Section 138 was, and is, necessary. To punish as a crime the failure to repay a debt – by use of Section 138 – cannot be the purpose of law. It is against public policy.

43 Coming back to fundamentals, the giving of a post-dated cheque implies that the drawer has no funds waiting in deposit to meet the cheque upon presentation. The cheque is a mere promise to discharge a present obligation on a future day. The fact of the cheque's non-payment when the due date arrives – without more – is no more evidence that it was given with fraudulent intent than is: (1) the permitting of a promissory note to go to protest as being proof of such (fraudulent) intent; or (2) the failure to pay the purchase price of goods sold on credit by itself evidence of fraud in the making of the contract. Fraud, it must be noted, cannot be predicated solely upon the mere non-performance of a future promise.

44 Stated simply, acceptance of a post-dated cheque amounts to advancing a loan, and the remedies for the non-payment of such cheques ought to be set forth in a Commercial Code (as civil remedies for debt recovery) and not in penal statutes where the punishment could be a jail term.

45 There are also several other ways to examine the real situation. First, in the ten-year period between 1980 to 1990, what was the instrument generally used[66] for securing a debt and on how many occasions was a post-dated cheque (which could be the subject of a suit under Order 37

66 The 'use' here refers to the initial use, in most of which cases the borrower pays the debt, leaving no need for a complaint to be filed. In other words, a criminal complaint is the culmination of the second stage when the cheque is dishonoured. The reference here is to the first stage.

CPC) used for securing a debt? And then, in the 10-year period from 1990 to 2000 (when these procedures became available), what was the 'increase' in the use of cheques as a mere security?–and the still further increase in the new millennium. The numbers will speak for themselves.[67]

46 Another way of looking at it is to ask: How many complaints were filed? How many complaints were found false? How many matters were compromised/payments made? How many drawers went to jail? and Of those who did go to jail, how many were cheats in the first instance or only those who had expected and wanted to pay, but had nothing left with them to pay? Once again, the numbers will speak for themselves.

47 The fear of being sent to jail for non-payment of a future debt often makes the debtor (and his family) do things which are best left unstated. Provisions on the likes of Section 60 of the CPC (exemption for specified assets of a debtor), insolvency laws and other humanitarian provisions all go to the wind. An element of a more humane approach has to be restored.

48 Section 138 was not meant to secure future debts. If that were so, then a new Section 138A could extend to all promissory notes, guarantees and every other form of credit instrument. Ought we to return to the day and age where a debtor unable to pay his debt was placed in jail? It is time that law found reform. Dishonour of the former variety of cheques (substitute for instant payment) be treated with greater sternness along with interest, sufficient costs & compensation to the payee, costs to the Court, fine to the State followed by (if it still remains unpaid) a jail term. A post-dated cheque, however, be taken out of the ambit of Section 138.

49 In this scenario, the right thing to do would be as under:

1 Keeping in view the intent and the purpose of the statute, and also reading it harmoniously with the Constitutional and other provisions, a post-dated cheque ought not to be included within the ambit of Section 138. Although such a result can be reached by a correct reading of the statute, even if it has to be read down, it must be.

2 If the provision cannot be so interpreted and has to be read as one providing punishment for non-encashment of a post-dated cheque, then, one may say with respect, the provision (in so far as a post-dated cheque is concerned) is unconstitutional, and be struck down. And;

3 Assuming it is held to be intra-vires (constitutional), for social and public policy reasons, a move for law reform on this score is a must.

Even in the Western countries, the dishonouring of a post-dated cheque is, absent other circumstances, not a criminal offence.

50 Consumerism is welcome, but to first lure people into purchase on credit, receive post-dated cheques as security and then one day, make them face

67 Once again, the 'numbers' here are for the cheques issued 'post-dated' as distinct from the number of complaints filed for post-dated cheques which were dishonoured. It is the 'use' of post-dated cheques as security for future payments which is to be deprecated.

the consequences of an erroneous expectation/judgment of being able to pay in future, is nothing but human exploitation. Law needs to develop a system by which the post-dating of cheques is treated as an evil requiring eradication and in that direction, law must take all necessary steps, including public education. However, to encourage and facilitate economy, a commercial instrument – a little more detailed than a cheque – and on the basis of which a civil court (DRT) Decree capable of execution can be passed forthwith, will serve the needs of securing debt / credit in the new millennium by use of the civil process as distinct from the criminal process. See para~ of Topic 2 at pp3~ supra.

51 What we really need is a separate statute that criminalises receiving goods / services against delivery of a worthless cheque and defines the other components of the offence. Seven days ought to be the limit between the date of delivery of the cheque and the date of its first presentation. The rationale is that some credit may be in the clearing and seven days is wide enough to cover what is a single transaction. Dishonour of such a cheque and failure to pay should – exceptional circumstances apart – result in a jail term, and not a mere fine. Topic 14 (sub-topic 3) of Chapter 10 argues how the tailoring of procedures in regard to dishonoured cheques (remaining unpaid after the statutory notice) can help speed up the judicial process.

52 A few words more. Cheques (as printed by the banks and given to their customers) are more or less of a standard design. This is necessary for convenience both in use and in the inter-bank clearing house. Here, a small innovation could be helpful. It is that in the standard cheque form (design) a box on the left (just above the cheque's number) be provided and a system of, preferably, writing the purpose/consideration for the cheque in a few words on it, can be put into practice and, in fact, encouraged.

53 For instance, a cheque given to a lawyer should either record 'professional fee' or 'advance for expenses', and not leave room, for a mischievous person (client), to later sue the lawyer for specific performance of an 'oral' agreement to sell his (the lawyer's) house by contending that this (cheque) was the advance money paid at that time. Recording the 'consideration' in this manner will not only prevent mischief and frauds, and save upon litigation, but, more importantly, also prevent tax evasion.

54 Then, as a practice, cheques are, on expiry of six months from the date written thereon, treated by the Banks as stale or out of date, and returned on that ground. According to the statute, there is no justification for such a practice; however, on the practical side – so as to prevent manipulations – the statute needs to provide a period of three months after which the cheque would be treated as stale or out of date.

☆ ☆ ☆

the consequences of an adequate expectation by the drawer of being able to pay in time [illegible] hundred [illegible] to develop a system by which the post-dating of cheques is [illegible] and requiring eradication and [illegible] in that direction, [illegible] all necessary steps, including [illegible]. However, to encourage and facilitate [illegible] a commercial instrument [illegible] little [illegible] from a cheque — and on the basis of which [illegible] can be [illegible] will serve the purpose of [illegible] credit in the new millennium by [illegible] the [illegible] process as distinct from the criminal process. See para. [illegible] supra.

1 What we really need is a separate statute [illegible] regarding [illegible] delivery of a [illegible] cheque and defining the [illegible] of the offence. [illegible] date ought to be the limit between the date of delivery of the cheque and the date of its first presentation. The [illegible] is that [illegible] and seven days is [illegible] to cover [illegible] a single transaction. Dishonour of such [illegible] cheque and [illegible] circumstances [illegible] and [illegible]. There is [illegible] how [illegible] measures in regard to [illegible] process [illegible] statutory [illegible] can help speed up [illegible] process.

2 A few words more: cheques [illegible] printed by the banks [illegible] to their customers [illegible] of a standard design [illegible] necessary for [illegible] both [illegible] and in the [illegible] clearing house. Here a small innovation could be [illegible] is that in the standard cheque form [illegible] on the left [illegible] the cheque [illegible] be provided and [illegible] preferably [illegible] the purpose [illegible] consideration for the cheque in a few words [illegible] encouraged.

3 For instance, a cheque given [illegible] record a [illegible] for [illegible] person [illegible] the [illegible] performance of an [illegible] agreement to [illegible] the cheque [illegible] consideration [illegible] will [illegible] and save much litigation [illegible] more important [illegible] also prevent [illegible] evasion.

4 Then, as [illegible] practice, cheques [illegible] validity [illegible] months from the date written thereon [illegible] and returned on that ground. [illegible] there is [illegible] such practice, [illegible] the statute needs to [illegible] period [illegible] after which the cheque would be treated [illegible] stale or out of date.

Justice, Courts and Delays

Table of Chapters

Chapter 9

The Role of Substantive law

Chapter 10
Criminal Law and Procedures

Chapter 13
Computers, Technology and BPR

Chapter 14
Towards a more efficient System

☆ ☆ ☆ ☆ ☆